John Lash was born in 1948 and spent his youth on ranches in Texas. He has studied and practised Tai Chi and Taoist thought for more than 31 years. In that time, John earned a Bachelor's Degree in Sociology at Texas A & M University, a Master's Degree in Philosophy at the University of New Mexico and completed two years of doctorate studies at the latter. During his personal spiritual journey, he has lived and studied with Sikhs, Hindus, Tibetan Buddhists and Jewish people, and on his travels he has visited the holy places of Islam, Christianity, Jainism, Buddhism and Native Americans. John lives on a farm near Berne, Switzerland with his wife and four children. He has been a teacher of Tai Chi for 10 years and operates the Harmonious Dragon Tai Chi School and White Crane Temple in Berne. John is the author of *The Tai Chi Journey* published by Element Books Ltd and *Cowboy Stories from East Texas*, a children's book, published by Hendrick-Long Publishers of Dallas, Texas, USA.

D0499413

This book is dedicated to my Tai Chi students,
Barbara Schmid, Annamarie Schwarzenbach,
Daniel Schärer and Vreni Hunn, who left for the Void
and took part of my heart with them

The Yin of Tai Chi

Tao, Tai Chi & the Mysterious Female

John Lash

© Vega Books Limited 2002
Text © John Lash 2000, 2002

ISBN 1 84333 615 4

British Library Cataloguing in Publication
data available

Published in 2002 by
Vega Books,
64 Brewery Road
London N7 9NT

A member of **Chrysalis** Books plc

Visit our website at
www.chrysalisbooks.co.uk

Indexing: Indexing Specialists

Printed and bound in Great Britain by CPD, Wales

Contents

Acknowledgements

I would like to thank all those who have taught me so much: my students; Charles Lin, my Tai Chi master; Betty Unterberger, who brought me onto the spiritual journey; Jean Sullivan, Tai Chi instructor in Memphis, who is a true Fairy Goddess; Urs and Monika Gauderon, who risked everything for freedom; Jamie Bloom, Tai Chi instructor in London, whose belief in this book made it possible; and Sri Dadubhai Patel, who has spent his life following in the footsteps of Mahatma Gandhi. All the passages from *The Tao Te Ching* are taken from the translation by Gia-Fu Feng, published by Random House, Inc., New York. Reading his translation is like listening to the stars sing.

Preface

A short time ago, I received a phone call from a man who said that he wished to learn the 'sport' of Tai Chi. A few days later, a student of mine told me that she had met a woman at a party who told her that she always had sport lessons on Tuesday nights. When my student asked her what sport she studied, she answered, 'Tai Chi'. She studied Tai Chi at an 'Oriental Sports School' directed by a Chinese man from mainland China who has done Tai Chi for decades. Needless to say, I was horrified and it was these incidents that determined me to write this book about Wu Chi.

Many Tai Chi students have probably heard the term 'Wu Chi' but have no idea of what it is, and yet Wu Chi is the very basis of the Oriental disciplines. It is the 'Ancient Beginning' that is the essence of the Tao and the Tai Chi journey. All of Tai Chi rests upon it and Tai Chi cannot exist without it. Without an understanding of Wu Chi, Tai Chi is but an empty shell, a toy for the bored.

☯ The Yin of Tai Chi

Wu Chi is the heart of Lao Tzu's teaching in *The Tao Te Ching* but it has not truly been examined in the last 1,000 years, so that today it is rare to find mention of it in any Tai Chi book or school. In probably the greatest work ever written on Chinese culture and philosophy, Joseph Needham's *Science and Civilisation in China*, there is barely a mention of it. In the few Tai Chi books that do mention the Wu Chi, such as Tsung Hwa Jou's *The Tao of Tai Chi Chuan*, it is only mentioned in passing and thus the reader is left without an understanding of the Wu Chi's centrality to Tai Chi. It is this loss of the concept of Wu Chi from Tai Chi teachings that has led to the degeneration of Tai Chi from its original development as a 'Way of Oneness' to its modern-day status of a sport or hobby. Once the student understands the nature of Wu Chi and its implications for his or her life, such a misunderstanding will be impossible.

Introduction

I have been on the Tai Chi journey for 31 years now and I have been a Tai Chi instructor for the past 19 years. I promised myself when I first began teaching that I would never have a school where people came merely to learn movements. The most horrible thing that I can imagine is to spend the rest of my life teaching people how to coordinate their knee with their toe. I decided then that I would seek to have a school where the students understood that Tai Chi movements are merely techniques to aid them in their journey to the Tao. The Tai Chi movements are nothing in or of themselves and are completely meaningless without a deeper grasp of the true meaning of Tai Chi. People think that they are doing Tai Chi if they are doing the movements correctly and the Tai Chi teacher aids in this illusion if he or she concentrates simply on Tai Chi techniques. In such a school, the Tai Chi student misses the overwhelming and awe-inspiring beauty of the Tai Chi life.

Lao Tzu says to teach 'no talking'. People tell me that speaking of the deeper meanings of Tai Chi is not necessary because by just doing the movements, the Tai Chi vision will mysteriously take hold of the student. That may be true in the Orient where every Chinese or Japanese child grows up with an understanding of the oneness that is the background in which they live, but this is not the way the average Westerner approaches life. Western people tend to compartmentalize their lives. Thus, it is continuously necessary to remind Western students of the oneness of all things. Anything we do, baking a cake, painting a wall, taking out the garbage, can be a Tai Chi movement and yet the West has developed no spiritual insights for disciplines centred around such mundane activities. For example, the West has had sword-fighting schools for centuries but has never developed a 'Way of the Sword'. We have been drinking tea for generations but have no 'Way of the Tea' ceremony. We have boxing but no 'Way of Self-Defence'.

We have no 'Way' (Tao) because our lives are lived in separate compartments. Our cooking lessons have nothing to do with our boxing lessons, which have nothing to do with the way we relate to our children, which has nothing to do with our professions. We exercise our bodies by going to gymnastic classes, we exercise our minds by reading good books and we exercise our spirit by going to church on Sunday. Never do our mind, body and spirit meet each other.

A 'Way', on the other hand, is a total approach to life in which the mind, body and spirit all participate equally and simultaneously. All the Oriental ways require this concentration of the student's being. Since the Western world never developed this concept of a 'Way', Westerners approach Tai Chi with the same separatist ideas with which they approach all else in their lives and thus they forfeit any chance of truly finding the 'Way' of Tai Chi. It is this 'total' approach to the Oriental 'ways' and especially to the Way of Tai Chi that is the purpose for the writing of my books. Just doing the Tai Chi movements will give the student exercise, improve his or her health and such like, but the inner vision must be passed on. Otherwise we ignore the struggles, pain, suffering and insights of all those journeyers to the Tao who came before us. Hence, despite the advice of Lao Tzu and others, I do talk of these deeper reaches of Tai Chi.

This book will not tell you about Tai Chi breathing or how to develop a perfect stance. There will be no discussion in these pages of the Five Elements, the *I Ching*, or the Animal Forms. You will not read of the Chi meridians or of Chi Gung exercises. There are many Tai Chi books that discuss these things which are all merely superficialities that simply work upon the student's ego unless he or she is deeply rooted into the ground from which Tai Chi sprang. Even the Tai Chi movements are superficialities without the Tai Chi vision. The Tai Chi movements express a story. They tell of the birth of the individual, the important stages of life, the responsibilities and duties each new stage brings and of the individual's return to the Void. Without the understanding of what the movements are expressing and this ancient story, Tai Chi is reduced to gymnastics or dance, which is why many dance schools list Tai Chi as one of the dances they offer.

The ability to do certain breathing exercises that will turn your aging face wrinkleless or put colour back into your greying hair, that will slow

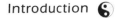

the aging process, that will enable you to push someone without touching them, that will enable you to leap great distances, are merely playthings, toys for the amusement and entertainment of the ego. They are only the glitzy outer aspects of the true hidden essence of what Tai Chi is. It is terribly unfortunate and sad that many people are attracted to Tai Chi by these things and never penetrate to the reality of Tai Chi.

This book, like the true Tai Chi school, has nothing to do with these superficialities but rather will seek to delve into the bare, pulsing, beautiful heart of the Tai Chi vision and provide for the true Tai Chi journeyer an understanding of the reality through which he or she is travelling and what this reality implies about his or her way of life. We live in a universe of Yin and Yang, of great suffering and great joy. Hopefully, this book will present to the journeyer an understanding of the Tao and Tai Chi that will give him or her courage to endure the suffering that comes into one's personal journey and the sensitivity to recognize the possibility of joy in even the darkest hour. Hopefully, the reader will see that in the true Tai Chi school, the heart of the teaching is not in the movements but in the sharing of the heart that occurs among the students and the teacher. By discovering and sharing the tenderness of each other's souls, the teacher and the students become the Tao in all its mystifying beauty.

That is why in my own school I refuse to allow people just to come and learn movements. With my heart and soul, I seek to break upon them like waves crashing against the rocks until their outer shells crack and their hearts come rushing out to join me in the eternal, fantastical, enraptured dance of the Tao.

Chapter I

Tao

Something mysteriously formed,
Born before heaven and earth.

VERSE 25

*The very highest is barely
known by men.*

VERSE 17

The truths of which this book speaks are not truths of the mind, which are but isolated facts. Rather, the truths of which I write are truths of the heart, truths which encompass all things. If you wish to understand what I say, you cannot examine the ideas I put forth under the spotlight of your rational mind but must, instead, open your heart and use it to feel each word for its softness, gentleness and beauty, caressing it as it whispers to your soul. Though your mind might laugh and ridicule the things written on these pages, your heart will know that it has touched upon reality.

First, I speak of the Tao, the Way, the 'Oneness', that vast pulsing ocean of Being and Non-Being in which all things exist and have their being. The Tao is a totality, a oneness that cannot be divided into its separate parts. Thus, nothing exists in isolation. All of us, every human being, every tree, every star, every mouse, every drop of water are part of each other and interdependent with each other. Nothing can be harmed without harming us all. Nothing can be loved without loving us all.

The Tao consists of two energies, the Yin or Female Chi and the Yang or Male Chi. These two energies flow through the universe like two great rivers, sometimes uniting in their flow and sometimes separating to follow different channels. When they meet and the two Chis combine, something is produced. Depending upon the combination in which they come together, a human being is produced or a rock or a butterfly. Thus, all things consist of Yin and Yang Chi and have both a female and a male aspect.

Hence, the Tao is a vast ocean in which all things exist. The waters of this ocean are the two Chis and all things, animate and inanimate, are fish swimming through the Chi currents. When we understand these things, we can attune ourselves to the flow of these currents and use them to dive into the depths or to shoot upwards toward the outer limits. Riding these Chi currents, we join the Great Harmony of all things and the universe sings to us its secrets.

So, here we are, fishes in this great ocean that eternally flows without purpose, without reason, without goal. It is an ocean in which struggle, strife and competition are useless. It is an ocean in which ambition has no place but where cooperation with and an appreciation of the value and beauty of each individual journey is necessary in order to attune oneself to the harmony of the whole.

It is an ocean in which each and every individuality is cherished for those unique aspects of its nature that allow it to contribute that which only it can contribute to the Whole. Every single rock, bird, star, human being, mosquito and blade of grass is cared for as if it were a cherished only child because each is absolutely necessary for the peace, tranquillity and harmony of all the others.

The Japanese have a very refined appreciation of this individual contribution to the harmony of the Whole. In the Japanese garden, each rock, shrub, moss and flower is contemplated with care and then placed in exactly the place in which its unique qualities will contribute to the harmony and beauty of a garden as a whole. Sometimes it requires 10 years to find the perfect place for a particular rock.

Like the Japanese garden, the Tao is a universe in which nothing is useless, nothing is wasted, nothing is without its own spectacular beauty. Thus to be a part of this harmony, people must hold each individual object, animal and person close to their heart. Hence, if there is someone or something that you consider worthless, it is you who have not been sensitive and discerning enough to see the uniqueness of its beauty. The beauty of the thing or person and its kinship to you is there if only your heart is tender enough to feel it. As the Tao (everything that is) cherishes you, so must you cherish everything that is.

Because you are its child, the Tao will never leave you. It is always there watching you with loving eyes, adoring and cherishing you and waiting for you with a mother's breasts and with arms opened wide. There is no escaping it, for you are in the middle of it and a part of it, just as it is in you as the arena of your being. All things sing the joy of your existence because through you and only through you will come their fulfilment in your nature's contribution to the harmony of the All.

The Tao is a great dance, full of laughter and smiles, in which all things want you as a partner. Tai Chi (the male aspect of Tao) and Wu Chi (the female aspect) combine eternally to call to you to leave behind your serious, gloomy, dark, isolated life and to join in the dance of pure being.

Chapter 2

Wu Chi

Knowing the ancient beginning is the essence of Tao.

VERSE 14

All things are composed of Yin and Yang Chi, the flowing waters of the Tao. Thus, everything has its Yin and Yang aspects. Yang Chi is masculine energy – strength, light, outward expression, Being. Yin Chi is feminine energy – soft, gentle, mysterious, inner expression, Non-Being. The Tao, as a whole, also has its Yin and Yang aspects. In its Yang aspect, it is Tai Chi, the outward expression of the Tao's inner nature. Its Yin aspect is Wu Chi, the Tao's inner nature itself. Hence, it is Non-Being, the female aspect upon which the Tao and Tai Chi rest.

Tai Chi is reality, Being, all that we see – trees, stars, rivers, people, animals, and so on. Wu Chi is the Void, Non-Being from which all Being arises. It is a principle of Western philosophy that *something* cannot come from *nothing*. But Taoist thought denies that principle and states that *everything* came from *nothing*. Thus, in the beginning, there was no Tai Chi, no existence, no Tao. There was only Wu Chi, Non-Being, and from this Non-Being came Being, Tai Chi. When Wu Chi and Tai Chi joined together in oneness, the Tao was formed. Because Wu Chi preceded Tai Chi and the Tao, it is the 'Mother' of all that is.

Before time was, before the coming of the seasons, before the coming of the change, before the emergence of the 'Ten Thousand Things', there was only the silent infinity of the Void, the great sea of Nothingness, Non-Being, the 'That Which Is Not'. It was from this infinite, silent Void, known in Chinese philosophy as the 'Wu Chi', that all things arose. Lao Tzu writes,

The ten thousand things are born of being.
Being is born of not being.

Verse 40

Taoist thinking presents the following picture:

First, there was only the Wu Chi (Non Being) which is Yin and is represented by

Then, the Wu Chi expressed itself in reality creating Tai Chi (Being) which is Yang and is represented by

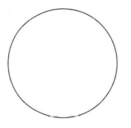

Wu Chi and Tai Chi together compose the Tao (Way) which is represented by

This design represents the constant movement from Non-Being to Being and back to Non-Being that is the eternal flow of the Tao.

Thus, everything comes from Wu Chi and is composed of Wu Chi. Your and my true nature, who we really are, is Non-Being, Wu Chi. It is the Wu Chi within me that links me in oneness with you and everything else in the Tao. The Wu Chi is the basis of our kinship, it is what makes me your brother. You and I are merely two different faces of the same thing, Wu Chi. Since the final destination of the Tai Chi journey is for the students to become one with the Tao (that is, with all things), it is essential that they find their own Wu Chi nature, who they really are, and dwell in its midst.

Being (Tai Chi) flowed from the womb of the Wu Chi (Non-Being) spontaneously without aid or direction. This movement from Non-Being to Being, from non-reality to reality is the primal movement of the universe and is the model for all movement. The flow from Non-Being to Being is what the Tai Chi person is seeking to become part of when doing the Tai Chi movements.

The creation of the universe was an unassisted birth. Such spontaneous action is, thus, the highest form of action and is referred to in Chinese as 'Wu Wei'. Wu Wei, spontaneous action, is the highest goal of all Oriental disciplines.

At the most advanced levels, practitioners of the Eastern Arts create their art by ridding themselves of the influences of the rational mind and ego in order to sink into their own Nothingness or Wu Chi nature where there is only silence and emptiness. When they have obtained this oneness with their inner self, the Wu Chi can flow and move through them in effortless unaided creation, exactly as the Wu Chi moved and flowed to create the universe.

In former times, Chinese and Japanese artists would sit in meditation for hours before beginning the process of painting. Only when they had become centred in the Wu Chi, when their minds were as still and clear as mirrors, their emotions calm and they were firmly established in the peace, harmony and tranquillity of their Wu Chi nature, would they reach out their hand to take up the brush. As their hand moved toward the brush, the creative process began. With the movement of their hand, they moved from Wu Chi to Tai Chi, from Non-Being to Being, from nothingness to reality. Since all things are united in the Wu Chi, the painter was one with the universe and it was the universe itself that flowed through them and expressed itself on the paper. Thus, the painter became, with the Wu Chi, a creator of the universe. Paper, brush, ink, artist – all disappeared and merged so that there was only the One and an observer could not say, 'They are painting' but only 'Painting'.

For the same reason, the Japanese swordsmith and his assistants would seek to reach the Wu Chi before beginning the sword-making process. The Sword Master and his pupils would retire to the hot baths, using steam and heat to purify themselves. Then they would don their immaculate ceremonial kimonos and sit in meditation for lengthy periods, reaching inward for the Wu Chi. Only when the master felt firmly embedded in the Wu Chi would he begin the 'ten thousand folds' of Japanese sword-making. As a result, these masters made the finest swords that the world has ever known.

This return to the Wu Chi before the movement to Tai Chi is attempted is essential to all the Oriental disciplines. The Tea Master seeks it before he begins Chano-u, the tea-making ceremony. The master of Ikebana, Japanese flower arrangement, seeks the Wu Chi in order to find the perfect harmony for their arrangement. And it is no less important for Tai Chi. The movements the students make become Tai Chi only when the students have first found their Wu Chi nature and have become rooted in it. This allows the Tai Chi movements to flow spontaneously from their natures. Without that rootedness in the Wu Chi which is the students' true essence, the movements are merely mechanical exercising of the body without meaning, mere gymnastics. But when the students are rooted in Wu Chi, the universe flows through them and creates reality (that is, Tai Chi).

The Void, or Wu Chi, is prized above all things in the Oriental martial arts because it is only in the Wu Chi that the defender is beyond danger in his oneness with all things – including his or her attacker. I have seen martial art demonstrations where two old masters would bow to each other and then remain standing in perfect stillness. After a while, they would bow to each other again and then walk away. Each realized that the other was in the Wu Chi and thus any move at all was pointless. If two things are one, how can they attack each other?

Hence, the Wu Chi is what all of the Oriental disciplines are based upon and directed toward and it is the Wu Chi that keeps them from being 'sport'. These disciplines were developed in order to help the practitioners into the vast ocean of Wu Chi that contains their own nature, who they really are, and to use it in their journey to oneness with themselves and the Tao. Thus, reaching the Wu Chi is the only valid reason for studying Oriental arts. Students who come to Karate in order to learn self-defence are missing the whole point of Karate and do not have the faintest idea of what Karate is. People who come to Tai Chi for exercise and good health are merely children looking for a new exotic playground.

Chapter 3

Non-Being

Thirty spokes share the wheel's hub;
It is the centre hole that makes it useful.
Shape clay into a vessel;
It is the space within that makes it useful.
Cut doors and windows for a room;
It is the holes which make it useful.
Therefore profit comes from what is there;
Usefulness from what is not there.

VERSE 11

The Wu Chi is the Void, the Emptiness, the Nothingness, Non-Being. This nothingness of the Wu Chi is the nature and essence of all that exists, just as the emptiness is the essence of a cup or window. However, when I say the Wu Chi is 'nothing', that does not mean that it is not 'something'. The term 'nothing' is used for the benefit of the rational mind which will never be able to grasp the true nature of the Wu Chi. That is why when reading this book, the reader must leave the rational mind behind. Where we are going the rational mind cannot follow. To the rational mind, something exists only when we can see it, feel it, taste it, smell it, touch it, hear it, in some way communicate with it or if we can somehow measure it

For example, let us imagine for a moment that there are small green people around us. There are thousands of them everywhere. They have cities and castles and they drive little green wagons pulled by little green horses to their little markets. Unfortunately, we cannot see them, hear them, touch them, smell them or taste them. They do not in any way affect our world and there is absolutely no way that we can get in touch with them. Yet, they are everywhere. One of them could be driving his little wagon right through me as I sit writing this. (Remember that no one knew of the existence of bacteria until they were revealed. So while little green people are highly unlikely, they are not impossible.) To the rational mind, these little green people do not exist. If something is imperceptible to it, then that thing does not exist. If I went around telling everyone about these little green people, I would soon be locked away somewhere. I would be seen as irrational (that is, insane). But, the little green people may really be there. Maybe it is only to the rational mind that they are nothing. If they do exist, they are nothing to the rational mind, but still, they are something. Thus, when I say that the Wu Chi is nothing, that does not mean that it is not something.

Another example would be if you had within you the focus, concentration, finger agility, coordination and ear for musical tones that give you the potential to be a great piano player. But, the great piano player does not exist because you have never tried to be one. I do not

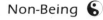

have the focus, concentration, finger agility, coordination and ear for musical tones within me that would allow me to be a great piano player. Thus, you have *something* I do not have even though that something has not been expressed. You are potentially a great piano player but you are *not* a great piano player. Therefore, there is no great piano player but there is something. Potentiality is *something* that is expressed in existence. It is not real but it is something. There is something there even though the mind cannot see it. The great piano player is unexpressed in reality and thus is unknown to us.

Hence, when I say that the Wu Chi is Non-Being, Nothingness, the Void, that does not mean that there is not something there. The Wu Chi is a potential something. In fact, as pure Non-Being, it is infinite potential. Now, it is a principle of the Tao that everything seeks to be real, to exist. Everything strives to be. That principle is obvious with any clear observation of the universe around us. The seed in the earth is only potentially a plant. In its drive to become real, it struggles to reveal and express itself to the world, pushing aside the dirt, seeking its way around the rocks until it finally bursts forth into the sunshine to exist in all its glory.

The caterpillar in the cocoon is only potentially a butterfly. The caterpillar strives toward reality, tearing apart its prison and emerging into the reality of butterflyness and in so doing, reveals its true nature to the universe. The sperm cell fights against almost impossible odds to find its way blindly to the ova in its search for reality. Along the way, thousands of other potential human beings are lost, never to emerge into reality. When the sperm is successful, the child begins to grow and struggles through the birthing process to emerge into the reality of true existence.

As a companion to this desire to be real, everything resists its own destruction. The rock will not simply fall apart and disappear because you do not like it. You must take a hammer and crush it. Against all odds, the mouse will turn to fight the tiger when it is cornered and has no place to run. Thus, everything seeks to exist in reality and to remain there.

Since this drive toward reality is a driving force in all things that flow

from the Wu Chi (Non-Being), it must be part of the nature of the Wu Chi itself. Hence, the Wu Chi seeks to express itself in reality. In other words, the Wu Chi seeks to move from Non-Being to Being. The potential piano player within you has limits upon its ability to emerge into existence. It relies upon you to have the desire, discipline and will-power to bring it into existence. If you lack that will and discipline, the great piano player within you will never exist. But, the Wu Chi is infinite potentiality and has no limits or constraints, nothing that it depends upon. Being free and infinite, it emerged into existence and the universe was created.

But why did the Wu Chi choose to express itself as the universe? Because, as we have already seen, true existence depends upon revelation. If the little green people do not reveal themselves to us, then they do not truly exist. They are mere phantoms floating through my imagination. Thus, Wu Chi created reality (Tai Chi), the universe, in order to reveal itself to that universe. With the creating of the universe, the Wu Chi has something real to reveal itself to. When this potentiality of the Wu Chi expresses itself in reality, Tai Chi occurs and the universe is created. Thus, Tai Chi is the act of bringing the potentiality of the Wu Chi, the Void, into existence. Tai Chi is the movement from Non-Being to Being. It is the Wu Chi creating itself.

Chapter 4

Love

The Yin of Tai Chi

Love the world as your own self...

Verse 13

38

Just knowing that the Wu Chi is pure potentiality is not enough for the Tai Chi student who must base his journey to the Tao on an understanding of the Wu Chi. The Wu Chi is potential, but potential what? The answer to this question lies in the Tai Chi person's realization that the Wu Chi created the universe and that the universe is a Oneness, a Totality, a Unity. Whatever the Wu Chi is, it is something that binds things together in oneness. There is only one thing in the universe that can make something one with another thing and the ancient Chinese sages tells us what that is. Love.

In the *Nei Ching*, written by the Yellow Emperor, Hwang Ti, and considered the oldest medical work in the world, illness is described as a condition that arises in human beings when the Chi within them ceases to flow. It goes on to say that the Chi ceases to flow when the patient has not *loved* enough. Now, let us remember that the Tao is an ocean of Chi energy in varying combinations of Yin and Yang Chis. Thus, the universe consists of continuously flowing Chi. What the *Nei Ching* is telling us is that *love* is responsible for this flowing, for the movement of

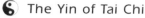

the universe and for all things within it. An understanding of love's role in the Tao is the cornerstone of the Tai Chi life, for it changes the way in which we look at ourselves and the world around us. Those who have reached this level of understanding realize that the sun rises because of love, the stars shine because of love, the grass grows, the river flows, the tiger attacks, the human pities, and your heart beats only because love is flowing. In other words, we live in and are surrounded by a loving universe.

Lao Tzu emphasizes the importance of love in *The Tao Te Ching* in Verse 67 when he says,

I have three treasures which I hold and keep.
The first is mercy. . .

By 'mercy' Lao Tzu means a deep feeling of compassionate love for all things. It is the compassion one feels when seeing a worm in the middle of the pavement on a rainy day. You pick it up and put it on the grass because there is an unconscious realization of your oneness with its life force and you would not see it die if you can help. Lao Tzu's 'mercy' is the deep sadness you feel when seeing children in poverty or someone confined to a wheelchair. It is the compassion that flares at the centre of your heart when seeing suffering of any kind. And it extends not just to conscious life but to all things. The same compassion overwhelms you when you see the forest being cut down or the rivers being polluted with chemical waste or the mountains being destroyed by ski resorts. (Of course, in Taoism, everything is conscious.)

The second and third treasures of Lao Tzu are economy and humility, but it is compassion that is listed first because without loving compassion there is no hope of oneness with others or of leading a life of Tai Chi. All the rest of Tai Chi (the movements, breathing exercises, meditations, self-defence, and such like) are merely playthings without this treasure of loving compassion. One can live a life of Tai Chi without ever learning a Tai Chi movement, but without loving compassion Tai Chi cannot exist no matter how long one studies the exercises. If the universe is composed of ever-flowing Chi energy and love is the cause of this flowing, then love is the means whereby human beings attune themselves to this universe. The Tao can only be approached with a loving heart. Hence, love is the most prized treasure of those who would seek the Tao.

But, abstractions such as the Tao are very easy to love. This type of love is Yang (male) love. The Dalai Lama, the Buddha and Mahatma Gandhi are examples of those who profess Yang love. They love all human beings, everyone who exists, because we are all children of the Spiritual Force. They love each human being *because* each is a human being. They love Lucy because she is a human being, not because Lucy is Lucy. They love Tom because he is a human being, not because he is Tom. They do not have to know Tom or Lucy in order to love them. They love their human beingness. Yang love is a necessity, otherwise we would be cut off in our isolated little groups of families and friends. We owe much to such exponents of Yang love as Gandhi, the Dalai Lama and the Buddha.

But, there is another love; Yin or female love. This love is a love of the mother for her children. It is face to face, soul to soul, body to body, heart to heart. In Yin love, I love Lucy *because* she is Lucy. I know her dreams, her visions, the pain she has suffered, her strengths, her weaknesses and the beauty of her individual soul. A mother does not love her child because it is a human being but because it is her child. And it is this type of love that binds us to the here and now.

The path of the Taoist is to save this Earth, to protect the Life Force. This was the example set by Lao Tzu who spent his whole adult life calling people back to the Ancient Way. It was and it is an impossible task. No one listens. Lao Tzu suffered the pain of seeing what war, the seeking of wealth and the development of social hierarchy was doing to people and to the Earth. In Verse 20 of *The Tao Te Ching* he describes his agony.

   . . . I alone am drifting, not knowing where I am.
   Like a newborn babe before it learns to smile.

I am alone, without a place to go.

Others have more than they need, but I alone
	have nothing.
I am a fool. Oh, yes! I am confused.
Other men are clear and bright,
But I alone am dim and weak.
Other men are sharp and clever,
But I alone am dull and stupid.
Oh, I drift like the waves of the sea,
Without direction, like the restless wind.

Everyone else is busy,
But I alone am aimless and depressed.
I am different.
I am nourished by the great mother.

Finally, when he could take no more hurt, he left through the Western Gate, the direction of the female paradise, Hsi Wang Mu's Magic Peach Garden, Avalon.

Before he was allowed to exit through the Western Gate, the Watcher said that Lao Tzu would first have to write *The Tao Te Ching*. Why? Because maybe in 2,000 years there would be another fool, such as John Lash, who would read it and decide to follow Lao Tzu's example.

So, I have spent my adult life calling people back to the Ancient Way, knowing that there is no chance. Sometimes I get depressed and filled with pain as I watch the Earth being destroyed. One night after a class, a student of mine told me I should not be depressed. If all life were to die out, in 100,000 years or so life would begin again.

Of course, I know this and it gives me some satisfaction. But, I have Yin love. It's good to know that maybe trees and animals and some types of people may live again but I love *these* trees in the forest around my farm. I love *these* people in my Tai Chi school and my family. I love *these* birds who eat at my birdfeeder. I want *these* to live and have the best lives possible. It is fine to love life in the abstract, but I love life in the reality, the here and now.

This Yin love is the love that is stressed by Lao Tzu in *The Tao Te Ching* and by the Taoist sage Chuang Tzu in *The Chuang Tzu*. Chapter 17 of *The Chuang Tzu* says,

Hold all things in your love. . .

and Lao Tzu writes,

The beginning of the universe
Is the mother of all things.
Knowing the mother, one also knows the son.

Verse 52

What Chuang Tzu and Lao Tzu are saying is that if you seek to be one with the Tao, you must become one with all of its parts. If love is what makes you one with the Tao, then it is love that is needed to make you one with each and every expression in the Tao. This is so because the Tao does not exist separately from its parts. Hence, I cannot in truth say that I love Switzerland but that I do not love all Swiss. And, I cannot say that I love myself unless I love my mind, my soul and my body, treating each aspect of myself with love. Hence, the Tai Chi journeyer must love every blade of grass, every person, every star and every mosquito if he or she is to unite with the Tao in oneness.

As a result of an understanding of the ideas of the ancient sages, we see that it is love that unites the 'Ten Thousand Things' into the oneness of Tao. This must be the case since it is only love that can make two things one. Of course, every mother knows this. While the baby is in her womb, the mother knows and feels the oneness with her unborn child. After the child is born, the doctor, science and the rational mind may tell her that she and the baby are now two distinct, separate beings but the mother knows that they are still one because her heart tells her so. That is why Lao Tzu continually speaks of the Wu Chi as the female or mother. He writes,

It is the woman, primal mother.
Her gateway is the root of heaven and earth.

Verse 6

and,

I am different.
I am nourished by the great mother.

Verse 20

The understanding of the role of love in the universe brings us back to the Wu Chi. As we have seen, Wu Chi is pure potentiality. Tai Chi is reality. Tai Chi is the result of the Wu Chi's expressing itself in existence. Since Tai Chi is thus born of Wu Chi, we can understand the nature of Wu Chi by observing the nature of Tai Chi (reality).

Reality, as we have seen, is united in oneness by love, flows with the aid of love and must be approached with love. Given the central importance of love, we see that love is the essence of all that exists, and all that exists came from the Wu Chi. With this in mind, the only possible answer to the question of what is Wu Chi is that it is potential love. The Wu Chi is love waiting to express itself in reality. The Wu Chi is a vast ocean of love waiting for the beloved. It is not real love but only potential love because it has not yet emerged into existence. When this love moves from potentiality into reality, it is Tai Chi. Tai Chi is love made real. Tai Chi is the expression of the Wu Chi's love and all things consist of the Wu Chi's love. Tai Chi is Wu Chi seeking reality. The universe came into existence through an act of love. The Tao is the universe loving itself.

But why did the Wu Chi create the universe? For an answer, we must remember the little green people. They are not real until they let us know that they are there. They must reveal themselves to us or forever remain non-existent. Love has the same problem. Love not expressed is not *real* love. In the beginning Wu Chi was all there was, but as potential love it needed an object to focus itself upon in order to reveal itself and to move into reality. The Wu Chi has the same drive for reality that we have already discussed as existing in all things. The Wu Chi thus had no other possibility for true existence except to create its one beloved in order to have an object to reveal itself to (that is, the universe). Hence, the universe was created in order to be loved.

Since all things come from the Wu Chi, Wu Chi is the nature of all things. Thus potential love is the nature of all human beings and everything else that exists. Because of this, the individual human being has the same problem as the Wu Chi (that is, how to become real). And we must follow the Wu Chi's example if we are to solve that problem. We must move from being potential human beings to being real human beings by loving. How much we express our love, how much we bring our loving nature into reality, determines how much we truly exist as human beings. To leave that love unexpressed is to remain a 'nothing', a little green person.

For example, I am sitting on the train going to work, reading my newspaper and you are sitting across the aisle from me. You are there behind the mask of your ego and I do not really see you. You are nothing to me. We are closed off from each other and as far as I am aware, you do not really exist. You are a 'little green person' to me. You may be there, but we do not in any way communicate, so what difference does it make whether you are there or not? You are no more real to me than the farms, houses and people passing by outside the window that I do not see as I read my paper. It is not until you stand up, cross the aisle to sit by me, smile at me with the warmness of your heart and speak to me, that I become aware of your existence as a real human being.

This need to express the love that is our nature in order to be real is the pure, uncovered heart of Tai Chi. And there is no escape from this realization. If you study Tai Chi for your health or to learn self-defence, if you consider Tai Chi merely a set of exotic movements and breathing exercises, you have missed the entire significance of this ancient discipline and are treating a precious jewel as if it were your toy. When we sink into our true nature and become one with it, our bodies, our thoughts, our actions, our world, our entire lives become expressions of the love that is the core of our being. By loving, we repeat the Wu Chi's act of creating the universe by creating ourselves. By loving, we reveal ourselves to others and bring ourselves into existence. Love is our means of communicating with all other things and we return the Wu Chi's message of 'I love you' with our own message of 'Yes, I know.'

Chapter 5

Pain

But I alone am drifting, not knowing
where I am.
Like a newborn babe before it learns to
smile…
… I alone am aimless and depressed.

VERSE 20

The universe is composed of, directed by and grounded in love and love is the nature of everything that exists. Because of this, the universe is a mystery and for ever beyond the reach of the rational mind. Thus, Lao Tzu says,

The Tao is forever undefined.
Verse 32

This is so because the rational mind cannot grasp the concept of love. Love is irrational. It has no logic and needs no reason. We love simply because our hearts demand it and the object of our love is not chosen by the mind. The rational mind cannot grasp an illogical concept. Hence, Tai Chi and the Tao must be approached with the heart rather than with the mind.

The result of our living in a universe of love is that life is indescribably sad and full of suffering. This is so because pain and suffering are inseparable from loving. Love is a feeling of oneness with the dreams, feelings and yearnings of others. It is a caring for the well-being of the beloved and a rejoicing in their presence. Our love reaches out from our nature to wrap the beloved in a golden web of light that binds the beloved to our tender, gentle and exposed hearts. In loving, we surrender ourselves to another and accept the possibility of great joy or crushing pain.

Suffering and love are inextricably bound together because of the nature of the Tao. The Tao is continual, never-ending movement and change. Everything arises from the Wu Chi, lives out its existence and then disappears back into the emptiness and non-being of the Void. Nothing lasts and there is nothing of permanence that we can cling to. This means that all that you love will inevitably be taken from you. The beloved will be ripped from the warm circle of your loving arms and carried away on the tide of change that ever flows back and forth through the vastness of the Tao.

Who do you love? That person could be leaving you right now. Even as I write these words someone I love could be dying. Do you love your children? They are growing up and already preparing to leave you. Thus, to love is to suffer.

It seems to me that no people have developed a deeper feeling for the sadness and fleetingness of life than the Japanese. The favourite time of the year for the Japanese is the Cherry Blossom Festival. During this season, the Japanese all seem to find the time from their busy lives to stroll through the cherry trees in order to view the flowering process, and in fact, one of the national symbols of Japan is the cherry blossom.

On the first day of the festival, the Japanese are filled with joy and pleasure in watching the buds open and new life and beauty beginning. The blooming of the cherry blossom is the symbol of newness, new beginnings and the continuance of life and creation.

On the second day of the festival, Japanese hearts are filled with wonder, awe and amazement at the overwhelming beauty as the flowers reach the heights of their beauty and glory, shining forth for all the world to see. The world is full of life and one can hear the singing of the universe at the joy and beauty of existence.

However, it is the third day that touches the deepest roots of the Japanese spirit, for it is on this last day that the cherry blossoms release their hold on life and, without a murmur of protest, drop in a flowery snowfall to cover the paths, to be trodden upon and ground into the earth. The blossoms cast away their lives, their beauty lost for ever. It is a time of exquisite sadness and aching to the Japanese heart because the entire Cherry Blossom Festival is a metaphor for life itself. The Japanese see their own existence and the existence of those whom they love through the experience of the cherry blossoms. We are all brought into existence in a burst of beauty, for what little child is not beautiful? Then we use our lives to shine forth in all our glory. But before we even realize it, life is past and we are falling back into the Void, casting ourselves at the feet of the world to be crushed and trodden upon. Life is so beautiful and so brief.

But why must pain, suffering and sadness be a part of a living universe? Because it is through pain and suffering and a recognition of the fleetingness of life that we gain sensitivity and sensitivity *is* life. We can only live and love fully if we are sensitive to the fact that that which we love will someday be lost to us. Only if we realize that life is rushing away from us will we see the absolute necessity to live every second of our life to the fullest, and since life is love, that means loving our beloved to the fullest.

I remember when the realization of the fleetingness of life really dawned upon me. From the age of 17 to 21, I was a student at Texas A & M University, which in those days was still mostly male and all military. My family were poor East Texas ranchers and the military would pay for your education at A & M in exchange for four years of service as an officer upon graduation. The first year was a nightmare of mental and physical pressure. Of the one hundred and fifty freshmen who began the year in my battalion, thirty-nine of us were left at the end of the year. Those of us who survived were extremely close because of our shared hardship. It was in my second year as a sophomore that I began to realize how much I loved A & M and its traditions. In the evening, as the sun was setting over the Brazos river, I would be at attention with my company, waiting to march to evening mess, watching the passing columns of cadets go by. I would see the young men in their pride and I loved them all. The Drum and Bugle Corps would be playing and the last dying, golden rays of the sun glinted off the sabres and the spearpoints of the guidons. One hundred years of history was marching by with its tales of battles and loss in war. The ghosts of all the cadets who had come before me stood before my mind's eye. It was all so beautiful and sad.

I was filled with a deep sadness that all this was passing away from me. Time was running out, the calendar was turning. Each day I woke up was another day closer to the end. In two years, all these young men who had shared four years of my life in our intimate little world on the Brazos river down in Texas, whom I had come to love so much, would go their separate ways in life and scatter never to be brought together again. Names would be forgotten, faces would disappear from our memories as we began careers, started families, and so on. All that would remain would be the glowing embers of the love that we had once shared. It was then that I decided that I must live fully every second of this wonderful and glorious time, that I must drink all the nectar from the beautiful flower of life, that I must love totally in the here and now so that when the loss and pain arrived, I would be wrapped in the warm layers of love buried in my heart.

What all this means is simply that if you are going to love someone you must love them now for they may not be here tomorrow. I live on a farm in Uettligen, Switzerland and I have four children. When they were younger, they had little hands with little fat fingers, and as I walked around the farm doing my work they liked to reach up and wrap their fat little fingers around one of mine. It was the most beautiful feeling in the world and I was always moved to deep love from their gesture of trust and oneness as I looked down onto their beautiful heads. They were so beautiful, trusting and innocent that it almost broke my heart just to look at them. But I knew even as I walked with them hand in hand that they were growing and soon I would never again have a little baby child who would wrap his fat fingers around my hand.

My wife always told me that when I was writing I should sit at the desk in the bedroom and close the door so that I could be alone and undisturbed. But I could not do that because I knew that my little children were in the living room and I did not want to lose even a second of their childhood. So, I would sit at the table to write, as I am doing now. I would sit here and write for 15 minutes or so and then my daughter would want me to help her with one of her little picture puzzles. I would leave my writing, help her with some pieces and then would sit down again to my work.

Ten minutes later, my little boy would want me to put 'Oh, Susanna' on the record-player and dance with him. So, I would get up, put on the record, then take his little hand in mine and we would dance around the room, celebrating the life that courses through his veins. I knew that I must not miss these things because some day they or I would be no more.

There is a man who lives up the hill in the village who has three sons who are four, five and seven. Every afternoon he comes home from work, turns on the television and watches sport shows, eats his supper and goes to bed. His wife called my wife the other day and asked if her boys could come once a week to my house and play with me. I was horrified. Here is this man watching television while his sons grow up out of sight and out of mind. Some day he will look around and they will be gone and he will be alone with his television, but then it will be too late to love. Such a man is completely insensitive to the needs of his sons for love and for the need of his own nature to express love.

How many times have you heard people tell you that someone they loved had just died suddenly and that they had never told them how much they loved them? Or, they had an argument with a friend and then the friend was killed in a car crash or something, and now they would never have the chance to heal the hurt that the argument had caused.

Those whom you love, you must love now. You cannot love someone and not tell them of your love. As long as your love is unrevealed, it is still in the Wu Chi and is only potential love. It is not real. Love unrevealed is not love at all. And, you must reveal it now for there may not be another chance.

It is the suffering and pain that results from all acts of love that are absolutely essential to the development of sensitivity within us and that open the way for our own nature. Suffering and loss teach us to treasure every second of life and open the flood-gates of our heart, allowing our love to pour out over those whom are beloved to us. It is the spur that makes us reveal our love to others in the 'here and now' because there may be no tomorrow. And, by revealing our love, we are like the Wu Chi revealing its love by creating the universe. As we reveal our love (the Wu Chi within us that is our true nature, who we really are), we create ourselves and become real human beings, truly alive because love is what life is.

Chapter 6

The Turning Point

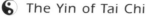

Between birth and death,
Three in ten are followers of life,
Three in ten are followers of death,
And men just passing from birth to death
also number three in ten.

VERSE 50

If I have even just a little sense,
I will walk on the main road and my
only fear
Will be of straying from it.

VERSE 53

When the realization comes into each of our lives that to love is to suffer because all that we love will be lost to us until we reach that ultimate loss, death, we are faced with a choice. Two roads lead away from this point of awareness. One road is the road of fear, a fleeing from love and the pain and suffering that love engenders, a fleeing from change, loss and death. The other road is the road of love. It is the road chosen by the journeyer who has decided to plunge ever more deeply into the life of love rather then fleeing it. It is the path that brings our Wu Chi nature into true existence, the path of making ourselves real. It is for those journeyers who have decided to follow the deep yearning that lies within themselves, to surrender to the infinite ocean of love that surrounds them, to flow with the living, flowing fountain of love that is their nature, to accept pain and suffering, loss and death as the price they must pay in order to reach the fulfilment of their true being, which is to become real, living, breathing, loving human beings. Which road we choose has tremendous consequences for individual lives, for the society in which we live and for the very existence of our planet.

Lao Tzu says,

Can you be as a newborn babe?
Verse 31

and,

Become as a little child once more.
Verse 28

Lao Tzu tells us this because children are born and live in oneness with their Wu Chi nature. In the womb, the baby is still in the Wu Chi. It is still only potentiality. In the birthing process it emerges into reality and the world of individuality. But, with no rational mind or ego to separate it from its Wu Chi nature, the child flows with the Wu Chi and remains one with all things. Its only motivation is to love and to be loved because this is ever the nature of Wu Chi. The child's first act after emerging into reality is to seek the breast and warmth of the mother where it lies and listens to the mother's beating heart, surrounded by her love.

Because the infant is still in its Wu Chi nature even though it has emerged into reality, it retains its oneness with the mother and the universe that it had when it was only in the Wu Chi. Thus the infant sees no difference between the toy it holds and its own hand because it relates to the Wu Chi nature of all that it touches, and the Wu Chi nature of the toy is the same as the child's own Wu Chi nature.

This ability to achieve oneness with all things is why all infants are beautiful and filled with the joy of life. To children, life is an adventure, a great discovery, and all things are magical (that is, unlimited by the rational mind). They have no rational mind to tell them that they are separate from their desires, hopes, dreams and wishes, that their visions are not real. They are one with their nature, which is love and compassion. They have not yet learned to look down upon others, not yet developed ambitions, and thus have not developed the ability to use other people unfeelingly as stepping stones.

Children approach everything and everyone with curiosity. Their minds have not yet categorized, labelled and dissected things and people, thus they perceive things and people as they really are. They perceive the uniqueness of all that they meet. They are as yet unfettered by the dry, rational, logical Western mind that turns the world into a dull grey, barren desert where souls die of thirst and hearts break in soundless agony for the beauty that they saw as children.

Adults know that there are no dragons, no elves, no Santa Claus, no Easter Rabbit, no Tooth Fairy, that cows cannot sing and pigs cannot fly. But the child does not know these things. It is not aware that there are limits because there are no limits in the Wu Chi. Thus for the child, all things are possible. Everything is strange and mysterious. The child is surrounded by mystery and that is why the child approaches everything and everyone with boundless curiosity. The child wants to explore the possibilities in everyone and everything. Nothing in its world is boring.

That is why the child can be fascinated with a rock and carry it around in its hand for hours, just experiencing its 'rockness'. Thus the child is like the 'Jian', the Oriental gardener. Both the Jian and the child seek to become one with the mystery of the rock's uniqueness.

The child uses its love and joy to explore every person it meets, ignoring the ego and going straight to the Wu Chi nature within that person. The child does not care if the person is Jewish, Buddhist or atheist; black, white or brown; 10 years old, 40 years old or 80 years old; rich or poor. It is only concerned with finding that place within all people where love, friendship and joy reside, because in that place it will find its playmate.

The child has as yet no fear of death and that is why its life is so full Adults would be bored to tears if they had no work to do or social functions to attend or some kind of entertainment. A two-year-old's day is filled to overflowing with things to do. It throws rocks into the dog's water bowl to watch the splashes, it digs holes in its mother's flower garden, it smears spaghetti sauce over its high-chair, it takes all the pictures out of the family photo album, it takes a nap, it pedals its little tractor around the house, and so on. In short, the child's life is full and it is never bored because its mind does not separate it from what it is doing. Thus, it is one with all that it does. Its love of life is evident in all that it does and it is ready to laugh and play at any second. It lives in the 'here and now'.

The ancient Mother World, the world of Tai Chi (that is, the world of the Wu Chi's love expressed), is the world into which we are born as children. That is why the infant is one with all things and sees no separation between itself and the world around it. Thus, the infant is like the rest of creation – the animals, stars and trees. All is mystery, all things are possible and there are no limits. The infant is one with its loving Wu Chi nature and exists in timelessness, living in the 'here and now'. The infant's heart is its guide through life, directing it toward love, warmth and nourishment.

Children become aware of pain and suffering quite early as they fall and skin their knees or cut themselves with the breadknife, bump their heads, and such like. But unlike the adult, the child does not flee pain and suffering. When the child is learning to run and falls, skinning its knees, it will cry, but the next day it is out running again. It does not stop running because of its painful experience but learns to run better.

Hence, the small child is a model for the Tai Chi person and that is why Lao Tzu advises us to return to the child-like state. Tai Chi people must, like the child, remain in their Wu Chi nature where all things are one while living in a world of individual beings. It is both the child's and the Tai Chi person's Wu Chi nature that makes them one with every individual thing or person that they encounter.

As time goes by, however, the rational mind begins to develop and it is a characteristic of the rational mind that it cannot see oneness but perceives everything as separated. Through the rational mind, the child experiences its separateness from the rest of the universe and thus loses its oneness with its Wu Chi nature.

As for myself, I remember waking up one morning in my room when I was 11 years old and it really hit me that I was going to die some day. Of course, I had known about death and I had known people who had died but this was the moment when I truly realized that death was my inescapable fate, also. I was terribly frightened and felt helpless and alone.

This realization of death as our ultimate end reinforces the feeling of separateness and aloneness. The child realizes that it and its family are not really one. If it were to die, its mother and father would go on with life, leaving it behind. Its parents are powerless to help it in its isolation. It must face death alone and in separateness. It is from this point that the individual first becomes aware of life as short and filled with dangers. And it is from this point that the individual begins to make those choices that will determine which of the two roads through life he or she will follow; the road of fear or the road of love.

Chapter 7

The Rational Mind
and the Road of Fear

 The Yin of Tai Chi

He who is attached to things will suffer much.
He who saves will suffer heavy loss.

VERSE 44

The world of reality is the world composed of love and compassion that came into existence when the Wu Chi moved from Non-Being into Being. It is the world that existed before Western society surrendered itself into the power of the rational mind; the world of oneness; the world of the Mother Tao; the ancient world of the Female. In this world that the Wu Chi created, humanity was only one aspect of the Wu Chi's love. There was no higher or lower. Humanity was no better or more deserving then rocks, deer, ants or stars. Everything was alive and full of spirit. Every tree, every rock, every animal, every star lived and flowed toward its own destiny in the great cosmic whole, watched over and guided by the loving female principle of the Tao: Wu Chi. In short, the universe was sacred and holy.

In using the term 'holy', I do no mean 'holy' as it came to be understood in religious philosophy but holy in its original meaning of 'complete'. Thus, a 'holy' man in Taoist thinking is quite different from a holy man in Christianity, for example. The Christian holy man is someone who is 'wholly good', someone who has rid himself of 'badness'. The Taoistic 'holy' man, on the other hand, is someone who has rid himself of nothing but in whom all things meet and develop a harmonious relationship. Rather than judging and rejecting, he accepts all things and all things meet in him. He is complete in that nothing is missing and everything exists within him in harmony, as in the Mother Tao.

Thus, something is holy and sacred when it cannot be added to or subtracted from without harming it. Hence, the only way to relate to a holy thing is to leave it alone, to refrain from interfering with it. That is why Lao Tzu says,

The universe is sacred.

You cannot improve it.

If you try to change it, you will ruin it.

Verse 29

This ancient, sacred Mother World that is the Tao was filled with mystery and wonder, a world of endless possibilities and endless discovery. It was the world of the child. Because it was a world of sacredness and infinite mystery, human beings had to walk through it very carefully. Everything existed in great harmony and no one knew what act might destroy the delicate balance of forces responsible for this oneness.

This idea is shown clearly in the Jewish experience. According to the Torah, God gave the Jews 613 commandments on how they were to deal with the world He had made. What God was saying to the Jews was that this is His world. He created it, all of it, and thus it is sacred. The Jew could not just do anything he wanted but had to approach all things as holy. Jews could not just go out and kill a calf for dinner. They had to be sure that the calf was killed in a certain way which was the most painless and merciful. God said that they could kill the calf but only if they approached it with loving compassion, Lao Tzu's treasure.

There are commandments for how to pray before eating because food is holy. There are commandments that deal with sleeping because sleep is holy. There are commandments that deal with using the toilet because all bodily functions are holy. The universe is holy and the Jew must approach every aspect of it with awe and reverence.

The same is true for Tai Chi, the world of reality created by the Wu Chi. To the ancient tribes, the Great Female Spirit resided in all things and all creatures. Thus, every insect, tree, rock, mountain, river and animal had the Mother Tao within it. If we observe the tribes that survived the destruction of the ancient Mother World, such as the Eskimos, the Pygmies and the Hopis, we see that they approach all of nature with magic and respect, with a sense of awe.

People could not simply walk up to a tree and cut it down. They had to approach the tree with a recognition that the tree was just as much a child of the Mother Tao as they were and that the tree had its own right to life and the fulfilling of its destiny. They had no right to take the life of the tree without first asking the Mother for permission. Perhaps of all the trees in the world, the Sacred Spirit loved this tree the most. Maybe this was the holiest, most beloved tree in the world. How was one to know? The Sacred Spirit is a mystery, also.

So, people had to approach the tree with awe and reverence, speaking to its Wu Chi nature, saying 'I am terribly sorry but I have to cut you down. I don't want to take your life but the winter is coming and I must build a shelter for my wife and children. I hope that your spirit has a safe journey to the spirit world, and when you arrive there, please tell the Sacred Spirit that I am sorry if I have offended It. Thank It for providing for me.' Only after seeking to placate the spirit of the tree and the forces that control the universe, would people cut down the tree and take it for their use.

Likewise, hunters could not simply go out and kill deer for sport or food. First, before the hunt, they had to ask the gods to help them in providing for their family. By notifying the gods that they were going to hunt, the hunters could assume that any animal they managed to kill was their gift to them. When the deer was killed, the hunters had to speak to the spirit of the deer, explaining why it was necessary to take its life, and ask that the spirit of the slain deer carry their message of thanks with it to the spirit world.

This female universe in which humanity lived teemed with life and sacredness. There were sacred rivers, sacred rocks, sacred mountains, sacred groves and sacred animals. And when, because of our awe and our gratitude, we celebrated this sacredness, the universe joined with us to sing the praise of the Mother, the oneness. We decorated the trees, we put flowers on the cows, we painted the elephants and we placed leaf boats with little candles on the river to be swept along by the current so that the river, too, could join in our celebration. In the old Mother World, humanity was not alone but merely one voice in the cosmic song of the living sea of love that is the universe.

The Wu Chi moved into real being when it created the universe and all things existed and had their being in the Wu Chi. The stars, the rocks, the trees, the animals – all existed in oneness with the Tao and all things existed in harmonious relationship with everything else. But there was no consciousness of the Wu Chi. Thus, there was nothing for the Wu Chi to reveal itself to, nothing to communicate its existence to, and so true existence eluded it.

With the development of the rational mind in the human animal, the Wu Chi's problem of revelation and communication was solved. With the development of the rational mind, there was a part of creation that was conscious of its own existence and aware of the vast universe around it. It was to this part of its creation that the Wu Chi could communicate its existence and reveal its nature of love and compassion. With the development of the rational mind and self-consciousness in human beings, the Wu Chi ceased to be a 'little green person'.

Unfortunately, there is a price to pay for self-awareness. With the development of the rational mind, we see our separateness. The oneness and timelessness of the Wu Chi is lost and we are left alone to face the world and death. The Eden of the Wu Chi's oneness, the old Mother World, is lost to us and like Adam and Eve, we have no place to hide.

The rational mind has made us self-aware and is horrified by the inevitability of death. The rational mind cannot see the oneness of the Tao but only the separate aspects of life and death. Because of its separating nature, it cannot see the connection between life and death but sees them as mutually exclusive opposites. The rational mind deals only with facts that can be examined, tested and placed into some kind of rational order and thus is completely at a loss in the face of mystery. Mystery is by definition that which is for ever beyond facts. The term 'mystery' does not mean the 'unknown' but the 'unknowable'.

Something is unknown if I do not know it but I could know it if I had all the facts. For example, the number of planets in our galaxy is an unknown. But, if I had a spaceship fast enough to travel throughout the galaxy and return to Earth in my lifetime, I could count all the planets and I would know.

But 'mystery' is for ever beyond facts and knowing. What is love? It cannot be observed under a microscope or seen through a telescope. It cannot be cut up and dissected. It cannot be reduced to numbers and put into mathematical formulae. You cannot hook me up to a machine with electrodes attached to my brain and decide when I am in love. What is death? Is there life after death? All of these are mysteries which the rational mind cannot touch upon.

Hence, the rational mind is most comfortable in the Aristotelian world of logic where two opposites cannot exist together at the same time. It cannot be both hot and cold outside. However, this Aristotelian logic can only be applied to measurable, physical facts, which is all that the rational mind can deal with.

In the world of mystery, opposites can and do exist together. We all know that within each of us is both niceness and meanness. Life and death are connected, interdependent and inseparable, but the rational mind cannot grasp this because it cannot comprehend oneness. Thus, death is a mystery which the rational mind cannot deal with. It is the recoiling from pain, suffering, loss and death that is the beginning of the road of fear.

Because no other part of creation has a rational mind (as far as we know), no other creature can lose its oneness with the Wu Chi. The loss of Wu Chi is a purely human condition. Our choice, as human beings, is whether to seek to recover the oneness of the Wu Chi by delving ever deeper into our loving nature or to surrender ourselves to the rational mind with its view of separateness and its overwhelming fear.

Chapter 8

The Surrender to the Rational Mind

Therefore the sage is guided by what he feels and not by what he sees.

VERSE 12

With the development of the rational mind, we become aware of our separateness, our individuality and the impending doom of that individuality in death. The rational mind can only see separateness and thus cannot understand that individuality and oneness can exist at the same time (that is, opposites existing together, Yin and Yang).

The fact that the Tao is a oneness of separate individuals cannot be grasped by the rational mind. Some people, rather than seeking to remain centred in their Wu Chi nature and using love to re-establish themselves into the oneness of the Tao, surrender to the rational mind's vision of total separation. They abandon the flow of their Wu Chi nature toward their destiny and seek to use the rational mind as their guide through life. This surrender has catastrophic results and in order to understand the inevitability of this catastrophe, we must take a closer look at the nature of the rational mind.

My being is a miniature Tao. All of the principles that operate in the Tao operate within me. If I wish to understand the Tao, all I need to do is look within myself. Thus, Lao Tzu says,

Without going outside, you may know the whole world.
Without looking through the window, you may see the
ways of heaven.

Verse 47

Like the Tao, my body is a oneness with all the parts playing a unique role. Everything goes harmoniously for me as long as all these parts fulfil their proper function. But, if one of the parts refuses to cooperate, the entire being suffers disaster.

For example, my feet have the responsibility of moving me around. They are a tool that my being uses for locomotion. As long as they fulfil this function, they are a blessing to me. However, if my feet were to start walking off of their own volition, or if they failed to respond to my will, deciding that they wanted to control the body, it would be a catastrophe for the entire being.

Like the feet, the rational mind is merely a tool. Its function is to solve problems. The nature of the rational mind is to separate. Separation is necessary in the process of problem solving. If I walk out to my car and it will not start, it does me no good if I only see the oneness, 'car'. I must be able to find the part of the car that is malfunctioning. The rational mind is superbly fitted for this task because it cannot see oneness. It automatically divides the whole into its parts. There are the parts that deal with electricity, parts that deal with air flow and parts that deal with fuel. I check and see that the fuel is OK and the air flow is good. Hence, there is something wrong with the electricity.

Problem-solving is the function of the rational mind and as long as it stays with this function, it contributes to the welfare of the whole. It is when the rational mind seeks to take over the function of guide through life that disaster occurs. Our true guide through life is our intuitive knowledge which flows from our loving Wu Chi nature which is our true self. I know that the universe is a oneness. How do I know this? I cannot say. I 'feel' it rather than 'see' it. There are no facts to support me, there is no logic to lead me to this conclusion. It is irrational and yet I know it is true.

If I live in a society that oppresses black people, there is no logical reason why I as a white man should object to it. There are reasons, however, why I should cooperate with this oppression. I have a family to support and as long as the blacks are oppressed, I do not have to worry that they will compete for my job. Rationally, it is to my benefit that they remain oppressed.

But, intuitively I know that these black people are one with me and that if I harm them, I am harming myself. This is a knowledge that the rational mind can never grasp because no matter what I say, my rational mind is going to see blacks as separate from me. To oppress people is wrong. I cannot tell you why it is wrong. Either you know it or you do not. There is no rational way for me to explain it to you because the understanding of why it is wrong flows from our loving Wu Chi nature and not from the rational mind. Suppression of others is a violation of love, which – as the potential of Wu Chi reveals – lies at the core of human nature. Therefore, when we treat another human being with anything other than love, we are not behaving as humans but are violating the essence of what it means to be human – which contradicts the core of our own nature and is therefore a violation of Tao.

With the surrender of our lives to the rational mind, we cut ourselves off from our loving Wu Chi nature and its intuitive understanding of oneness; the rational mind is left to direct our lives without interference from that part of us which makes us one with all things.

Death is a mystery, and it is death, pain and suffering that the rational mind most fears. Thus, the rational mind must flee from death and seek to deny it. In denying the mystery that is death, it must deny all mystery. It is as if I were king of America. I cannot allow Texas to tell me that it wants to exist outside my rule. If I allow that, perhaps California or Ohio will also want to be free. People who surrender to the rational mind make the rational mind the king of their lives. If the rational mind accepts that there are areas of life beyond its control (mystery), then its rule is threatened.

The world created by the love of the Wu Chi, the old Mother World, is all mystery. The Tao is a oneness like my body, and like my body, every individual part has a unique nature and a unique role to play. Every rock, person and animal has its unique destiny in the great Whole. What the uniqueness is is a mystery, and that is the mystery that the Jian gardener is seeking to grasp with his Wu Chi nature as he reaches out with his love rather than with his mind to touch upon the essence of the rock in his garden. All these unique parts of the Tao are interdependent and nothing works if even one of these parts is not fulfilling its role. But the rational mind rejects mystery and cannot perceive the uniqueness of individual objects.

Mystery can only be known by becoming one with it and love is the only thing that can make two things one. Barbara is special, unique. There is not another person in the universe exactly like her. To know Barbara, I must become one with her uniqueness by loving her.

A thing that is mysterious must be approached with caution. We do not know what it is, thus, we do not know what will harm it or frighten it away. The approach to mystery must be made with exquisite gentleness and softness. In other words, mystery must be approached as a lover approaches the beloved. When I seek to know Barbara, I must reach out to her softly and tenderly with the love that flows within my Wu Chi nature, delicately and sensitively feeling for that place within her where my Wu Chi nature can touch upon hers. When the contact is made, we are one and she is revealed to me in all her beauty.

Everything in our lives must be approached in this manner. Everything is unique and precious. There is no such thing as good or bad; only harmonious and disharmonious relationships. If I have trouble with someone, it is my fault because I have not found the place within them where we meet in oneness. The Tai Chi person's life is a continual effort to establish a harmonious relationship with everything that exists.

Since the rational mind cannot deal with individuals in their uniqueness, it creates categories in order to be able to keep all of its isolated facts together and to make them easier to handle. For example, the rational mind has the category 'female' and it has a list of characteristics of what femaleness is. It also has categories of '40 years old' and 'English'. Hence the rational mind does not need to get to know

The Yin of Tai Chi

Elisabeth because according to its categories, it already knows all it needs to know about her.

It does not matter to the rational mind that Elisabeth may not be at all like the categories say she is. Elisabeth could be, and is, unlike any other 40-year-old English female that the rational mind has ever encountered, but that does not matter. The rational mind must make Elisabeth fit into its categories because it cannot understand what it is that makes Elisabeth Elisabeth and not someone else. It can dissect Elisabeth, put every cell in her body under the microscope, but it will never be able to discover the uniqueness of Elisabeth.

This means that the rational mind can only deal with Elisabeth as the representative of a category, an object, something plastic and separated from itself, and ultimately boring since there is nothing it can perceive that is unique about her. The only way to understand who Elisabeth is, is to become one with her. The only way to understand mystery, such as uniqueness, is to become one with it, just as the Jian is seeking to do with the rock in his or her garden. But this process of becoming one with something is impossible for the rational mind because of the rational mind's separating nature.

Because of this boringness of Elisabeth as the member of a category, the rational mind treats Elisabeth the same way it treats a rock. The rational mind thinks it knows all it needs to know about rocks. It has seen millions of them in this life and they are all the same. They are hard and they just lie there. Rocks are very boring things to the rational mind. If it sees a rock lying by the side of the road, it is bored by the rock and wants the rock just to stay out of its life. It knows what this rock is like and it wants nothing to do with the rock unless it can use the rock in some way, because when the rational mind becomes separated and dominating it becomes utilitarian.

People may pick the rock up and throw it at a dog that is trying to bite them, or they might put it in front of a tyre on their car to keep the car from rolling down a hill. They do not care about the rock. As soon as they are through with it, they will throw it out of their way, not even looking to see where it lands.

The rational mind treats people the same way. On Saturday night, the young man goes to a bar and sees Nancy leaning against a wall. She is pretty and he is sexually aroused. He thinks Nancy is very boring because he has seen a lot of 20-year-old women and he knows what they are like. All he needs is sexual relief. He is not interested in what her childhood was like, what her dreams are, what her occupation is, what makes her sad or happy, or why she happens to be standing in a bar on Saturday night all alone. All he wants is to use her body for sex.

If he succeeds in getting her to go home with him and have sex, the next morning he wants her to leave as soon as possible because she is boring and he has things to do. He got what he wanted and now she is useless to him. There is no difference between her and the rock he used to block the tyre on his car. He is in no way concerned whether she has been harmed by his use of her.

This is how the rational mind works in the world. It takes what it needs from everything it meets and then casts it aside. The epitome of the rational mind in action is science. Science requires the scientist to remain separated from that which he studies. Thus, the scientist dissects the frog to see what useful facts he can learn without caring about the harm done to the frog.

As a result of this rational approach toward the universe, we use everything we meet in life, and when its usefulness is over, we cast it aside with no regard to any harm we might have inflicted upon it. We dig ore out of the earth and leave gaping holes behind and we dump waste into the rivers. To the rational mind, the world is an empty soda can.

Thus, the rational mind destroys the ancient Mother World of Tai Chi that was created by the Wu Chi because it is unable to perceive the unique Wu Chi nature that is the essence of all things and which unites all things into oneness. Instead, it destroys their uniqueness by putting all things into categories according to physical facts.

The sacredness of the universe is destroyed by the rational mind. Trees no longer have spirits but are reduced to mere hunks of wood to be cut down en masse in order to make space for a car park. Animals become mere hunks of moving meat to be slaughtered for food or killed for sport. Rivers become globs of water that carry off our wastes. People too become mere hunks of meat which we hope will stay out of our lives unless we can use them in some way.

With the surrender to the rational mind as a guide through life, we doom ourselves to a life of separation and isolation in a dead world. The world of the Tao in which we were born, a world that was filled with mystery and where all things were alive in their own spirits, is lost and we are alone on a dead planet in the centre of a dead universe. When we lose contact with our Wu Chi nature and surrender to the rational mind, we lose our sense of the sacredness of the universe. And, Lao Tzu says,

When men lack a sense of awe, there will be
    disaster.

Verse 72

Chapter 9

The Ego

There is no greater sin than desire,
No greater curse than discontent,
No greater misfortune than wanting
something for oneself.

VERSE 46

When we surrender our lives into the power of the rational mind, we must reject all mystery as the rational mind seeks to flee from the mystery of death. But, all the important things in life are mysterious – oneness, uniqueness, love, beauty, friendship, death and such like.

In the Tao all things are interdependent with everything else because all things must cooperate in order to establish the harmony of the Whole. Hence, the existence of the Tao, the oneness, depends upon each and every thing fulfilling its unique role and destiny. If even just one part is missing, then the oneness is lost. If all creation cooperates in harmony but you are missing, the Tao is lost for us all and there is nothing we, the rest of creation, can do but wait for you to join us. This makes you the most important person in the universe. The entire universe is waiting for you to do that which you have to do, that which only you can do, and we are helpless without you. The Tao depends upon you.

All things have the Wu Chi nature at their centre but there are variations of that nature. Certain variations make a tiger. Others make a tree and yet others make a human being. The nature of a tiger is strength, power and ferocity. The nature of human beings is compassion and mercy. And both the ferocity of the tiger and the mercy of the human are expressions of the Wu Chi's nature. The ferocity of the tiger helps to keep the number of deer in harmony with their environment, thus contributing to their ability to continue as a species. The mercy of the human allows us to be a force for the binding of the universe with strands of love.

In the human aspect of the Wu Chi nature, there are more variations. Every human being's nature has its own unique qualities that make that person who he or she is and not someone else. It is this unique nature that is your being, your essence, and it is the fulfilling and revealing of this uniqueness that makes you so vitally important to the universe. The revealing of this nature, who you really are, is what moves you from Wu Chi (potentiality) to Tai Chi (reality).

But, the Wu Chi, inner nature, uniqueness and Tao are all mysteries and the rational mind rejects mystery. Thus, with the surrender to the rational mind and the resulting loss of our oneness with the Wu Chi, we stand alone, cut off from who we truly are, to face the overwhelming and terrifying power of an alien universe, a power that will some day crush us. It is the Wu Chi nature within that links the person to the oneness of all things, and when this link is cut the person feels unimportant and helpless, a mere insignificant speck in the vast cosmos.

It is the rational mind that causes us to lose our oneness with the Tao but it is powerless to give us a new oneness because its very nature is separation. The rational mind cannot see that death is a return to the Wu Chi potentiality. All things must face death; nothing but the Tao lasts for ever. Death is part of the Tao and by separating out death in an effort to reject it the Tao ceases to exist, because if even one piece is missing, the Whole is lost. By trying to deny death, we separate ourselves from the common destiny of all existence and our lives become meaningless. How can life have meaning without death? How can joy have meaning without sadness?

To give our isolated, separated lives meaning, the rational mind creates the fiction of the 'Ego'. The ego is our excuse for existence in a meaningless world. It tells us that we are important not because of some unique, mysterious inner nature, but rather, because we are white or rich or educated or Christian or American or from a good family, and so forth. The development of the ego by the rational mind completes our separation from the Wu Chi. It is the wall we build around ourselves to keep meaninglessness out. The ego tells me that I am important simply because I exist and the only meaning in life is the fulfilment of my desires and ambitions.

As stated before, life is full of sadness, pain and suffering because all that we love and cherish will ultimately be lost to us. Nothing remains as the Tao flows onward. The ego seeks the fulfilment of desire and the avoidance of suffering. In order to avoid suffering, the ego must reject love. If I do not love you you cannot hurt me when you leave me. Thus, the ego builds a wall around me to keep you out.

Our feeling of separation disconnects us from the Wu Chi, our development of the ego entrenches our separation, and the ego's development of internal walls to keep love out makes that separation permanent. Only if our inner being is touched by love and compassion, only if the love of our Wu Chi nature is allowed to flow freely can we again become one with the loving universe that the Wu Chi created, but it is exactly this free flow of love within us that the ego makes impossible.

The Wu Chi had to express its love in reality before it could become real. Thus, we must allow our love to flow from potentiality to reality before we can become real. With the building of a wall by my ego to keep you out, I have imprisoned my own loving Wu Chi nature. Since my Wu Chi nature cannot express itself in reality, I cease to be real. Without the expression of my Wu Chi nature through loving, I am not a real human being but only a potential human being. And, because my ego will not allow your love in, you cannot express your Wu Chi nature to me, which means you can never be real to me.

The butterfly exists inside its cocoon until it reaches a certain stage of development and then bursts forth in all its beauty and glory to live briefly and then to return to the Void. Its beauty touches our hearts and makes the world a nicer place to be. People who follow the road of fear refuse to be like the butterfly, to follow the way of all things. They build a cocoon around themselves and refuse to come out because if they come out they must face death eventually. Thus, they never enter the reality of humanness. Their beauty and glory as a unique aspect of the Tao is never seen by the world. They seek to avoid the pain and suffering that come with true existence.

But, the Tao cannot be changed. Opposites cannot be separated no matter how much the rational mind tries. Trying to avoid pain and suffering, people dominated by the rational mind increase the amount of pain and suffering in the universe because they do not let their love or the love of others express itself, and without this expression of love there can be no joy. In their effort to avoid suffering, they have lessened the total amount of joy in the world and increased the total amount of suffering.

They do not want to see pain and suffering, so they seek to wall it off by surrounding themselves with luxuries. Since they are cut off from a feeling of oneness with Nature, they do not care that their desire for luxuries destroys the world around them. They do not care that their luxury car pollutes the air, or that their desire for fur destroys animal species, or that their desire for a gold wristwatch tears up the Earth.

Seeking to avoid suffering, they do all that they can to avoid change and growth. Change is frightening because change occurs in time and time leads to death. Because they have lost the timelessness of Wu Chi, they have entered time. They are for ever running out of time because their death is ever drawing nearer. They have only 70 years of life, so they really have to hurry. They have no time to be a Jian gardener contemplating a stone, seeking to touch upon its unique essence, no time to learn the tea ceremony or Tai Chi, no time to relate to the uniqueness of things, people or even themselves.

As a Tai Chi teacher, I see this time obsession of the ego quite often. People call me and ask me how long it will take them to learn Tai Chi. I usually suggest another Tai Chi school to them because the answer in my school is 'eternity'. People who are in a hurry because they only have 70 years have no time to learn true Tai Chi.

Because they have to hurry, people who live in time have no patience. Time is racing by. They must have something to fill the empty spaces of their lives so that no time is wasted. They must have entertainment, something to keep the senses occupied. They must avoid silence and tranquillity because in silence and tranquillity the mind automatically turns inward and they do not want to see the emptiness and meaninglessness that exist within themselves. Thus, they go through life with a radio plugged into their ears so they can exist in solitariness without having to relate to others. They sit alone at home watching television, not realizing what entertainment does. Lao Tzu says,

The five colours blind the eye.
The five tones deafen the ear.
The five flavours dull the taste.
Racing and hunting madden the mind.
Precious things lead one astray.

Verse 12

What Lao Tzu is saying is that entertainment of the ego leads one away from the reality of the inner self.

This is the world of ego that the rational mind has created, a world of isolation and numbness, a world where everything is dead. The people who live in this world are as dead as the world that surrounds them. Change, growth, experience, love – these are the definitions of life and it is these that the person who has surrendered to the rational mind and the fiction of the ego rejects. Thus, in seeking to flee from death, they are actually rushing toward it. Everything is a toy that only exists for their entertainment. They do not avoid the fate of the cherry blossom, they only lose the beauty and the burst of glory as they pass through this life as flowers that never bloomed.

Chapter 10

The Way of Tai Chi and the Road of Love

Therefore the truly great man dwells on what is real…

VERSE 38

There is a road to life other than that followed by the rational mind and its fictional creation, the ego. It is a road that runs through the world of reality, the world of Tai Chi, and it leads us back to our source, the Wu Chi. Tai Chi is the Wu Chi's love made real. Thus, the world of Tai Chi is reality and all else is mere illusion.

All of the Oriental disciplines were developed in order to help the practitioner to regain his or her Wu Chi nature which was lost with the development of the rational mind and its view of separation. With the regaining of our true self, our Wu Chi nature, the illusion of the ego and our isolation are destroyed. Piercing this illusion, we can return to the ancient Mother World where all things are alive and filled with spirit as they dance together the Cosmic Dance of a loving universe. Making the universe live again is the essence of all Oriental arts – the Tea Ceremony, Yoga, Tai Chi, Karate, Aikido, and such like.

As we have seen, life is full of pain and suffering and the reality of death is always present. We realize that all we love will be taken from us and that this loss can occur at any second. People who follow the road of fear reject this pain and seek to isolate themselves from loving and being loved. Such people understand that they can only be hurt if they love. They seek to hold you at arm's length, to keep you from coming too close, because if they allow you to come close they will love you. They will love you because you are the most beautiful thing in the universe, pure loving Wu Chi nature. Their own loving Wu Chi nature will automatically reach out to you to reforge the oneness between you that was lost with their surrender to the rational mind.

Such people's great mistake is that the rational mind they have surrendered their life to follows its separating nature by seeking to separate opposites. Opposites can be separated in the world of physical facts but not in the world of spirit. Suffering and joy, life and death, cannot be separated. The rational mind seeks to reject the pain that comes with loving but in so doing it also rejects the great joy that comes with loving and being loved, and of living in a loving ocean of being. By trying to reject death, it rejects life, which is love expressed. It cannot see that the opposites of oneness and individuality exist at the same time.

Physically, we are individual and separated, while in our Wu Chi nature we are one.

But there are some people who take a different path when they encounter pain, suffering and loss. Realizing that those whom they love can be snatched from them at any second, rather than seeking to cut themselves off from love, they rush headlong toward love, seeking to love the beloved even more because every second is precious. This second may be their last opportunity to make the beloved aware of their love.

The path back to our Wu Chi nature and oneness with the Tao is long and arduous, filled with both great pain and great joy. The first step on this journey is to put the rational mind back into its proper place as a problem-solver rather than a guide. It is the rational mind that fears death. Without the rational mind's control, the fear of death disappears. The baby in the womb is comfortable, at ease, without pain. It floats and swims in the warmth of its mother's womb, hearing the lulling rhythm of her heartbeat. It knows nothing of the world that awaits it outside the mother's womb yet, when it is time to go, the baby shifts its body for the journey and endures the hardest struggle it will ever face in order to come out into the world, to obtain reality. It has no fear because it has no rational mind. It is time to go, so the baby goes. That is the 'Way'. With the taming of the rational mind, the Tai Chi person passes out of the womb of life in the same fearless manner into the unknown of death.

All the Oriental disciplines concentrate on this taming of the rational mind with its sense of separation and fear. Zen uses 'Koans' or sayings which the practitioners are to concentrate upon with their minds. These Koans contain opposites and contradictions that the mind cannot separate, such as 'What is the sound of one hand clapping?' When the mind becomes exhausted from its efforts to understand, the Wu Chi nature of the student is able to burst through in all its glory and 'satori' or enlightenment is achieved.

In Yogic practices, the mind is focused between the eyes and the consciousness is turned inward through meditation until an awareness of the Wu Chi nature is obtained. In Tai Chi, the mind is placed in the 'Tan

Tien', a spot three inches below the navel. The Tan Tien is the point where body, mind and spirit meet in oneness. Here, the mind is stilled and the Wu Chi nature can come to the fore and assume its role as guide through life.

The two different roads that lead through life have produced two different worlds that exist together in the same place at the same time. The road of fear runs through the world of ego, a dead world full of lifeless people, a world of ambition, fear, competition and isolation. When the journeyer has tamed the rational mind and become centred in his or her Wu Chi nature, he or she leaves the world of ego and enters the old Mother World of Tai Chi where everything is special, alive and beloved. The world of ego is a fictional world, as fictional as the ego that created it. The Tai Chi world is reality, the Way, the Tao. Hence, when the journeyer is centred in his or her Wu Chi nature, they enter the world of reality and become real. They create themselves.

In the world of ego, death is loss, a horror, an extinction that can occur at any second. People who live in this world lead meaningless lives and die meaningless deaths. But in the world of Tai Chi, death is completely different. As we have seen, all things are unique. The pen I am writing this with is different from any other pen in the universe. There is not another one exactly like it. It is an aspect of the Wu Chi. It has some special role to play in the great harmony. In other words, it has meaning. Its existence means something. What that uniqueness is, what its meaning is, I do not know. It is a mystery.

It is the same for people. We are unique and have a special role to play in the oneness of all creation. What that role is we do not know and the purpose of the Oriental arts is to help us find that destiny. Unless we each fulfil our purpose, our destiny, the Tao will be lost. If all things find oneness and harmony but you are lost, then none of us will succeed. That makes each individual thing that exists the most important thing in the universe. The entire universe needs you to do what your nature needs to do in order to fulfil itself. The universe is vitally concerned with your progress through the Tao. Thus, when you find your Wu Chi nature and flow with it toward your destiny, the universe flows with you.

Lao Tzu says,

> When you are one with the Tao,
> The Tao welcomes you.
>
> **Verse 23**

When you have obtained oneness with who you really are, the universe will allow nothing to happen to you until the destiny of your Wu Chi nature is fulfilled. Hence, Lao Tzu says,

> He who knows how to live can walk abroad
> Without fear of rhinoceros or tiger.
> He will not be wounded in battle,
> For in him rhinoceros can find no place
>   to thrust their horn,
> Tigers no place to use their claws,
> And weapons no place to pierce.

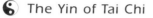

Why is this so?

Because he has no place for death to enter.

Verse 50

The universe will not allow such a person to die until the unique Wu Chi nature of that person has fulfilled itself and added its unique contribution to the harmony of the Tao. Like the cherry blossom, the person in the world of nature plunges into the stream of life that flows out of the Wu Chi, bursting forth in all his or her beauty and glory to move our hearts, and only then falls at our feet to return to the Wu Chi mother. Lao Tzu says,

Be the stream of the universe.

Verse 28

Thus, people who live in the world of Tai Chi, the world of reality, the world of love, live lives filled with meaning. They write the story of the

Tao with the actions of their lives. Their lives tell the story of the Wu Chi's love, its struggle to exist, and the peace, harmony, and tranquillity that lie within the Tao's embrace. Death, when it comes, is the final chapter of the story and they must approach it with the same love and appreciation with which they approached life, for both death and life are aspects of the Wu Chi's love. Death is the final chapter, the last line in the beautiful story of love that Tai Chi people write with their lives.

To me, the greatest example of such a life was that of Mahatma Gandhi. His life was a story of love, compassion and non-violence; a fearlessness toward death. The death he died at the hands of a fanatical gunman was the perfect ending to the story of his life. If he had not died in such a way, people would have wondered if he could have held to his beliefs in the face of destruction. He proved the meaning of his life by dying with his hands clasped in the traditional Hindu greeting of love and with words of sacred awe upon his lips.

When we enter life, we leave the total oneness of the Wu Chi and emerge into our individual existence while remaining one with all things through that part of the Wu Chi that is our inner nature. We are sad and suffer because all things are temporary and all that we love, which for the Tai Chi person is all things, will be lost to us. But it is this suffering and sadness that allow us to feel sympathy and compassion for all things because we share a common fate. Calmness and joy come to us because we know that the nature of all things will survive in the eternity of the Tao.

Lao Tzu writes,

Though the body dies, the Tao will never pass away.

Verse 26

He goes on to say,

The beginning of the universe
Is the mother of all things.
Knowing the mother, one also knows the sons.

**Knowing the sons, yet remaining in touch with the
mother,
Brings freedom from the fear of death.**

Verse 52

What Lao Tzu means is that the Wu Chi is the mother of all things. Everything came from the Wu Chi and if we know the Wu Chi, we know 'the sons' (that is, the nature of all things). We have always existed in the vast ocean of potential love that is the Wu Chi. When we came into life, we emerged into our individuality while remaining one with the All through our Wu Chi nature. Knowing life and the world and seeing our individuality but 'remaining in touch with the mother' (that is, remaining in our Wu Chi nature) gives us freedom from the fear of death because we realize that death is merely a returning to our original state of pure oneness, floating in the warmth and love that is fluid in the womb of the universe. With this overcoming of the fear of death, the journeyer is prepared to live the life of Tai Chi.

Chapter 11

The Tai Chi Life

Therefore the sage takes care of all men
And abandons no one.
He takes care of all things
And abandons nothing.

VERSE 27

Each of us is a perfect miniature of the Tao. All that exists, exists within us. The principles that operate within the Tao, that move the planets in their orbits, that spin the galaxies through space, that cause water to seek the lowest path, are all present within us. Hence, the life of Tai Chi (love made real) is a life of imitation. Just as in the Tai Chi school the student imitates the movements of the teacher, so the Tai Chi journeyer imitates the movements of the Tao.

The Wu Chi, seeking reality, moved. It expressed its love in reality by creating. Its love congealed into the universe. This movement from Non-Being to Being, from potential love to real love, is Tai Chi. Thus, the Wu Chi presents us with the example of how the Tai Chi person must live his or her life.

Tai Chi journeyers must first find and root themselves in who they really are, their Wu Chi nature. They must rid themselves of the ego and 'find' themselves. But, simply to remain in the Wu Chi is to be only a potential being. Journeyers must reach out with their Wu Chi love and touch the universe. By so doing, we make ourselves real as our love is expressed in reality and we create ourselves and those whom our love touches.

Returning to the strangers-on-a-train analogy, you are 'nothing' to me and I am nothing to you. I do not know or love you. You are but a figment of my imagination, a shadow flitting past my mind. I appear the same to you. It is only if I stop you and reveal my love to you that I see you as real and you see me as real. My Wu Chi nature will have revealed itself to you and used its love to touch upon you. By loving you, I make myself real, just as the Wu Chi made itself real by loving the universe. The Wu Chi created the universe by loving it into existence. I make you real by loving you into existence.

This is not only true of people but of inanimate objects, also. My youngest son had a little teddy bear. To me, it was just a piece of cloth filled with stuffing, an inert thing that really meant nothing. But, to my son, it lived. It had a spirit of tranquillity, warmth and peace. When we put my son to bed, he tossed and turned restlessly until we brought him his teddy bear. He hugged it to himself with his love for it and soon he was touched by its spirit of calmness and slept. To him, the teddy bear was not just a lifeless piece of stuffed cloth to be thrown out of the way, but a special companion and friend whom he loved dearly. My son made the teddy bear live. He filled it with spirit and gave it meaning by touching it with his love.

To Tai Chi people, the whole world is like my son's teddy bear. They must do for the entire world what my little boy did for a piece of cloth with stuffing. We must touch the trees with our love so that they are again the sacred groves of the old Mother World, we must touch the rivers with our love so that they once again are filled with spirits that chuckle as they pour over the rocks, we must touch the Earth with our love in order to transform it into the Mother of us all. Only our love will heal our wounded planet.

Just as the teddy bear became something that could not be thrown into a corner out of the way, so our world will become a place we cannot destroy with our poison. We must reach out and touch people with the love that is our Wu Chi nature so that they will not spend their dead lives in a dead universe. Tai Chi people must love all that they meet and in so doing create them, using their love to bring them into reality. Our love re-creates the Mother World; the world that flowed from the heart of the Wu Chi; the world that is Tai Chi; the world of love expressed.

Everything is an aspect of the Wu Chi's love. Everything has a unique beauty and a unique role to play in the universe. This uniqueness is mystery. It is this uniqueness that the Tai Chi person seeks to know.

Hence, the Tai Chi person is the Jian, the Oriental gardener, of the universe. The Jian will spend 10 years seeking to become one with the uniqueness and the special place in the Tao of a particular stone in his garden. Once he has found and become one with the uniqueness of the stone, he places it in exactly the perfect place in his garden where its unique beauty will be shown in all its glory, in perfect harmony with all the other objects in his garden.

Thus, the Jian constructs a miniature Tao in which everything exists in harmony with everything else and where the unique nature of every object fulfils its special destiny. It is a garden where the beauty of the individual enhances the beauty of the Whole and the beauty of the Whole enhances the beauty of the individual.

This is the way of Tai Chi people. They seek to become one with the unique nature of all that they encounter, to aid and to nourish them so that they can fulfil the destiny of their unique nature, and to help them find that special place in life where they can exist in harmony with all others. The Tai Chi person is the Jian and the universe is his or her garden.

All of the Oriental arts are centred upon helping the student to acquire the ability to obtain oneness with the surrounding environment. In the Tea Ceremony, the practitioners seek to obtain perfect harmony with the bowl, the fire, the stirring whisk, the movement of their own clothing, and such like. In so doing, they make them live and allow their spirits to emerge, thus filling the practitioner's world with meaning.

People dominated by the rational mind, on the other hand, heat some water, throw a tea bag in the cup and gulp it down while reading the newspaper. To such people, the cup, the water, the tea, are all dead things, separated from them. These things are merely aspects of the dead world in which they live. They drink their tea in isolation, not even consciously aware of the objects with which they are dealing.

When the Tea Master makes his tea, he finds the Void within that is his Wu Chi nature and allows his love to flow out to touch upon the tea-making objects. He thus becomes one with them in a loving, harmonious relationship. He, the cup, the tea and the fire are all being real together; they are doing Tai Chi together. When the Tea Master drinks his tea, the universe has a cup of tea with him.

In Tai Chi, we go through the same process as the Tea Master, but rather than using implements for making tea, we use our bodies and our fellow students. The Tai Chi student seeks to become one with their own body, with each part of the body existing and moving in perfect harmony with all the other parts of the body and with their body moving and existing in perfect harmony with the bodies all of the other students.

People in the world of ego have no time or patience for such endeavours because life is short and they must hurry. They have no time to live and experience. They are separated from Wu Chi, the Void, where there is no time. Because the Tai Chi person is rooted in the timelessness of the Wu Chi, there is no hurry when acting in the present for there is only the eternal 'now' where the future and the past meet and mingle. Lao Tzu writes,

Stay with the ancient Tao,
Move with the present.
Verse 14

Thus, the Tai Chi person has 10 years to contemplate a rock and seek to touch upon the mystery of its uniqueness. He or she has time to make the universe live. The Tai Chi person has eternity.

Chapter 12

The Tai Chi Person in the Two Worlds

Yielding is the way of the Tao.

VERSE 40

Tai Chi people live in the world of nature, the loving world created by the Wu Chi, the world of reality (Tai Chi). By rooting themselves in their own Wu Chi nature, they become one with the universe of love that is the world of reality. Their nature flows forth, creating their path, and they become 'the stream of the universe', a flowing river of love carrying them toward their unique destiny. By allowing their love to flow forth, they become real and everything they touch with their love becomes real. With the fulfilling of their destiny, they fulfil the destiny of the Wu Chi. They are a doorway through which the potential love of the Wu Chi enters reality, Tai Chi.

Tai Chi people must also move through the world of ego, that fictional world created by the rational mind's fear, a world filled with unreal people and dead things. This is the world that the great majority of people inhabit and this is the world that Tai Chi people are bringing love and reality to.

The ancient Tai Chi saying, 'Stand like a mountain; flow like a river', describes how Tai Chi people exist in these two different worlds. In the world of ego, Tai Chi people 'flow like a river', which means they yield. The river flows around the rocks in its path rather then seeking to smash their hardness. It yields to the strength of the stone and yet, with time, its continuous flowing motion wears away the hardness.

The people who live in the world of ego are separated from their Wu Chi nature and its love. They are like stones in the river of our journey. They have built walls around themselves to keep us out. Like the river, we yield to this hardness; the hardness of their opinions, their ambitions, their desires, their frustration and anger at living in the prison they have created for themselves. But our Wu Chi nature is continuously sending its love to wash over them and gradually the flow of our love erodes the walls within which they have isolated themselves.

There is no other way to penetrate the ego's walls. Force only increases resistance. Trying to struggle with such people with our opinions and arguments would only increase the thick-ness of their walls. Thus, Tai Chi people are like the small child. We ignore the categories established by the rational mind and the ego. We do not care if the person is black or white, rich or poor, liberal or conservative, Christian or Moslem, capitalist or communist. We ignore all these walls of separation and continuously seek to pierce them with our love, to touch upon that place within them where we are united in oneness; the Wu Chi.

Such a life requires that Tai Chi people possess a certain quality that Lao Tzu stresses over and over again in *The Tao Te Ching*. He says,

Be one with the dust of the earth.

Verse 56

Accept being unimportant.

Verse 13

and,

I have three treasures which I hold and keep.
The third is daring not to be ahead of others.

Verse 67

and,

Merge with dust.
Verse 4

Humility is essential for living the life of Tai Chi. The importance of Tai Chi people lies in the world of nature, the world of reality. They are important because they are unique aspects of the Wu Chi and have a unique role to play in creating the harmony and peace of the Tao. No other can do what they must do. No other can take their place. All of creation waits for them to fulfil their destiny, for without them, the universe is helpless and the harmony of the Tao is forever beyond reach.

But, in the world of ego, Tai Chi people are totally unimportant. It is a fictional world where there is no meaning, no reality. So, what does their opinion mean in such a world? They have no ambition to fulfil, no need for achievements to enhance their self-prestige, no need for the respect and admiration of others for the meaning of their existence.

The meaning of their existence lies within themselves, untarnished and undamaged by the judgement of others. They have nothing to defend.

At one time, I had an elderly neighbour who lived a life of total isolation. He was filled with anger and pain because he was cut off from his Wu Chi nature and unable to express the love that was his true being. He would stay inside his house and brood, filling himself with anger at life until finally he would reach a point where he would have to let the anger out.

One day, as I was coming back from the barn, I saw him in the yard, yelling at my wife. I walked up to him to see what was wrong. He then began yelling at me. It was something about my four children making too much noise when they were playing outside the day before. Sometimes I forget that I am a Tai Chi man and on that occasion I became angry and thought, 'He has no right to talk that way to me'. But luckily, I remembered who I was. Why doesn't he have the right to talk to me that way? This is the world of ego, the world of illusion, and in this world I am nobody. Let him yell. How can it hurt me since I am in

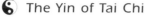

the womb of the Wu Chi?

This man must let his anger out on someone and who better to yell at than a Tai Chi man whom his anger cannot harm? If he yells at someone of the world of ego, there will be a fight and resentment. I am lower than the dust, a nothing in the world of ego, totally unimportant. My love can drain all the poison from his anger until it is spent and exhausted. I will yield and yield until his anger is spent.

Thus, I apologized to him for the problems we had caused him and told him that we would try to do better in the future, all the while sending my love toward him, ignoring his ego, searching for the love within him that must respond. Finally, his anger was drained from him and I knew everything would be all right for another month or so until the anger within him had time to build up again. Over a period of years, his walls toward us eroded away and he became friends with us.

With humility, we flow like the river. I can go down to the Aare, the river that flows by the city of Berne, Switzerland, and I can yell at it and curse it all day. 'You call yourself a river. You are nothing. The Mississippi, now there is a river. You are just a little nothing of a stream. The Nile, the Rhine, ah, these are something.' And so I can go on, but the Aare does not care. It has no ego, nothing to defend. It flows serenely on its way toward its destiny, which is to merge with the ocean, yielding and flowing around the hard objects in its path, gradually wearing them down. It nourishes all that it meets, helping things to grow, and it is completely immune to criticism or praise. It flows silently onward, making claims on none. Hence, Lao Tzu writes,

The highest good is like the water.
Water gives life to the ten thousand things
    and does not strive.
It flows in places men reject and so is like the Tao.
               Verse 8

and,

Be the stream of the universe.

Verse 28

and,

Tao in the world is like a river flowing to
the sea.

Verse 32

I was explaining the necessity of being 'one with the dust' to one of my
Tai Chi classes one day when one of my students objected. She said that
if you lived that way, people would humiliate you. But humiliation is not
something that comes from outside yourself. It is something that must
come from within. How can anyone humiliate you? Can anyone
humiliate the Aare? Humiliation is merely a sign that the Tai Chi person
has not yet rid herself of the ego and merged with the dust. Humiliation
means 'to make humble'. How can you humble someone who is already
humble? Only the ego can be humiliated.

In order to flow like a river in humility, Tai Chi people must rid themselves of opinions. Lao Tzu says,

The sage has no mind of his own.
Verse 49

Opinions simply separate us from others. They label us and categorize us. They build a wall between us and others so that others cannot see our true selves. For example, when I was 25 years old, I worked as a gardener in a hotel in England. There was an English man who worked there also, who was one of the most gentle, open, loving human beings that I have ever met. Everyone loved him, and in the evenings, friends would gather around him just to be near such love and warmth. None of us knew if the others were leftists or conservatives, Jews or Christians, capitalists or communists. Our conversation never turned to these areas because in the face of love these things seemed unimportant. The only thing that was important was to be near this man.

Later, he went to New Zealand for some months. When he came back, he was a radical leftist and he was intent upon telling everyone how the world should be run. All of his friends who were not leftist left him. Now he lives with a small group of radical friends who spend hours exchanging radical ideas. Where once he really had a chance to change people and the world through the example of his love, now he is isolated and completely ineffectual in his efforts to make the world a more loving place, all because now he has an opinion that separates him from others and keeps him from being able to deal with others on the heart-to-heart level.

The world of ego is a fictional world. It is not real and has no meaning, so what use is it to have opinions about what happens in a fictional world? What difference does it make what kind of government we have – communist, dictatorship, democracy, theocracy, and so on? If there is love and compassion among the citizens and between the government and people, the type of government is irrelevant. If a dictator is loving and compassionate to his people, nourishing them and helping them to reach their full potential, guiding them toward love and non-violence, rooting them in the concepts of peace and respect for the Earth, who would not rejoice at having such a ruler?

But, if the government is composed of men and women simply seeking to fulfil their ambitions, using the divisions of society for their base and support and not basing their actions upon love and compassion for their citizens, what does it matter if they call themselves Socialists, Communists, Fascists or Democrats?

The destiny of Tai Chi people is to puncture the wall others have built around themselves with the love of their Wu Chi nature, to make the love that lies within the true selves of others respond to their love, thus helping others to discover who they really are. Giving opinions about the fictional world these people inhabit threatens their ego and makes them thicken the walls they have built around themselves. If you are a radical leftist and I start giving out conservative opinions, you will immediately shut yourself off from me and now we can no longer communicate. Any chance we had of touching upon the true essence of each other is lost.

☯ The Yin of Tai Chi

As I write this, the conflict between NATO and Serbia drags on in Kosovo. One night, one of my students asked me, 'What do you think about the situation in Kosovo?' I knew this student was very pro-NATO. That same night, I was taking the bus home when a Serbian friend of mine sat beside me and asked me my opinion of the Kosovo conflict. I knew that he was very pro-Serbia. Both of them received the same answer. I told them that I really did not know what was going on, that I did not watch television or read the newspapers, so I really could not give an opinion. I am sure they both think I am stupid but they are not angry at me. I am a nice stupid guy. Lao Tzu said, 'I am a fool'.

I try to live in the world of nature and in the world of nature the view of the Kosovo conflict is completely different from that in the world of ego. In the world of ego, people try to talk to each other without having tried first to become one with the other's hopes, dreams, fears, and such like. This kind of talking is called 'diplomacy'. People run around the world trying to solve problems using diplomacy. They behave like the doctors who treat symptoms of the disease while ignoring the disease itself. It is as if I went to the doctor because my leg hurt and he gave me a crutch.

The Tai Chi person sees that the disease is our isolation from each other and our inability to love. You can talk all day about Islamic fundamentalism, Western values, Milosevic and so on, but all of these are mere symptoms and arguing about who is right or wrong is senseless.

My 16-year-old son asked me why they are fighting in Kosovo. I asked him if he could shoot me. No, he could not. 'Could you shoot Mother?' No. 'How about Grandfather or Grandmother?' No. 'Why not?' I asked. He could not because he loved us was his answer. Exactly. They are killing each other in Kosovo because they do not love each other. Forget all the rest, Christianity, Islam, democracy, human rights, and so on. They do not love each other and the wars and killing will not stop until they do.

Hence, the Tai Chi person has no opinion on the symptoms but deals only with the disease. Tai Chi people use their lives to do the only thing that can be done and that is to spread their love and compassion over the world. Thus, Lao Tzu writes,

> **Blunt the sharpness,**
> **Untangle the knot,**
> **Soften the glare,**
> **Merge with dust.**
>> **Verse 28**

In other words, have no opinions because their 'sharpness' cuts people who are passionate; untangle the 'knot' of intellectual argument; soften the 'glare' that turns others away from you and 'merge with the dust' of humility, realizing that you are totally unimportant in the world of ego. Let all your actions and dealings with others not be driven by opinions in a fictional world but rather, rest in the reality of your loving Wu Chi nature which understands the true cause of war, hate, envy, poverty and environmental destruction – the lack of love.

The only way to teach anyone about anything is by example.

All parents know this. I can preach and sermonize all day to my children, telling them to show love and compassion to others, but if I do not set an example with my own life, they will know that all my words mean nothing. The Tai Chi person follows the example of the Wu Chi. Students learn the Tai Chi movements by following the example of the teacher. And Tai Chi people must provide an example for the world. They must show the world the joy, peace and tranquillity of a life lived in a loving and harmonious relationship with all people and all things.

Lao Tzu says,

Know the white,
But keep the black.
Be an example to the world.
Being an example to the world,
Ever true and unwavering,
Return to the infinite.

Verse 28

White is the colour of Yang, reality, the 'Ten Thousand Things'. Knowing the white means to understand why people desire glory, fame and wealth, why they are ambitious and competitive and why they feel anger, jealousy and envy. It is understanding how the world works. People who 'hold' to the white are alone, separated from who they really are and are lost in the yearnings of the ego.

Knowing the 'white', the Tai Chi person keeps to the 'black'. Black is the colour of the Yin, the female principle, the Wu Chi. By keeping to the black, we keep to humility and the female principle of life based upon love and compassion. Lao Tzu is saying that we should remain in our Wu Chi nature while living in the world of reality. By keeping to the black, we become an example of what human life was meant to be and we return to our Wu Chi nature which is infinite love. Demonstrating, fighting, arguing and getting angry will change nothing. Tai Chi people feel pain and suffering as they observe the unending cycle of destruction occurring around them – the crushed lives, the loneliness, the poisoning of Nature, the religious and racial hatred – but they must realize that they can only change things by becoming an example of what the world was meant to be.

The love of Tai Chi people will cause a response in even the most hardened heart. I have never seen love fail if pursued fully. It may take time to see success but Tai Chi people have time because they live in the eternalness of the Wu Chi. Love is the true nature of all humans and love must respond to love. Hence, Lao Tzu says,

All men come to him who keeps to the one,
For there lies rest and happiness and peace.

Verse 35

Tai Chi people become the loving Earth Father or Earth Mother who accepts all things and all people as their children. With their tender hearts filled with compassion, they continuously and gently touch upon the hearts of others, calling them home to the ocean of tranquillity that is the Wu Chi. This is the meaning of 'flow like a river'.

'Stand like a mountain' is the principle upon which Tai Chi people live in the world of reality, the world created when the potential love of Wu Chi flowed into existence, the world of Tai Chi. In the world of the ego, Tai Chi people flow like a river, yielding and yielding and yielding because they have no ego to defend and no ambitions to fulfil. But in the world of reality, the Tai Chi person cannot yield but instead must 'stand like a mountain'.

As the river flows through the world, it nourishes all things, giving benefit and life to all it touches. Though its waters are so valuable and essential, still it seeks the lowest places in humility and asks for no acclaim or recognition. It yields to all who come to it, giving itself without question or judgement.

However, if you seek to violate the principles of its nature, its reality, the river will kill you. If you jump into the river with lead boots on, it will drown you. Not because it wants to but because that is the nature of water. It cannot yield without ceasing to be water. It cannot choose whether to drown me or not. Whether I am a saint or a murderer has no relevance. When its nature is violated, the river 'stands like a mountain', unyielding.

Tai Chi people are like the river. They are ever yielding in the world of ego, seeking to wear down the hard places in their path with their love and nourishing all that they meet. But there comes a point where the Tai Chi person can no longer yield.

In ancient Taoist tradition, there are nine magic words used as a means of self-protection. They are called the 'Shuji Shuriken' in certain Japanese Buddhist sects. The last word is 'Zero' and it means the point at which the Way no longer operates. It is the point where the way of yielding can no longer be followed.

'Zero' is reached when someone seeks to violate the Tai Chi person's nature of love and compassion. The Tai Chi person yields and yields until he or she reaches that point where the way of yielding no longer has power. For example, let's say that the government passes a law that all Jews will be put into concentration camps. I will yield to their anger at the Jews. I will listen to their tirades while sending forth my love in an effort to pierce through their heart, to arouse their awareness of their true Wu Chi nature. But, if I fail and they come to take my Jewish neighbours, then I have reached Zero.

It is my failure that I have reached Zero because if I had loved enough I would have succeeded in taking away their hostility toward Jews. I have failed to 'flow like a river' and now I must 'stand like a mountain'. I cannot allow them to violate my nature of love and compassion. I would cease to be John Lash. First, they must overcome my resistance. My loving Wu Chi nature will not allow me to stand aside as they harm my neighbours. And that is why the Tai Chi movements are also a form of self-defence.

If Tai Chi people are in a position where others try to force them to hate others, to separate them from their way of love, to make them agree to the mistreatment of their fellow human beings or Nature, then they have reached 'Zero' and can no longer yield. In the world of reality, Tai Chi people 'stand like a mountain', unmoving and unyielding. Nothing will be allowed to interfere with their flowing journey to their loving destiny, not even death, for their journey will continue beyond death and beyond time.

In the book *The Ugly American* there is a scene where an American is trying to escape pursuing Japanese soldiers in Burma and he runs into a Buddhist temple. He looks for a place to hide. He sees two monks sitting before a great gold Buddha, meditating. Hearing the soldiers coming, he hides behind the Buddha. The Japanese soldiers come in and approach the monks. One puts a gun to the head of one of the monks and asks him where the American is hiding. The monk is aware of the question and of the imminence of death but he is flowing in his Buddha nature through the cosmos and refuses to be moved from this harmony and peace, who he truly is.

The Japanese soldier shoots the monk in the head and the monk falls forward, his blood splattering on the robes of his fellow monk. The Japanese approaches the other monk and puts the gun to his head, repeating the question. This second monk was aware of all that had happened, including the death of his friend, but nothing was going to move him from his Buddha nature and he did not answer. The Japanese were disgusted and ran on. The point is that the monks were in their Wu Chi nature and nothing, not even death, was going to make them violate their path. They were at 'Zero' and could not yield.

Thus, in times of catastrophe, when storms rage in the ocean of life, Tai Chi people become the mountain standing in the midst of the swirling waters upon whom others can cling because Tai Chi people are unmoving and unchanging. When the world is collapsing around them, they are an island of tranquillity, harmony and peace where, as the loving Earth Father or Mother, their children can seek comfort.

Someone wants to beat a child? I am sorry. This is 'Zero' and the Tai Chi person cannot allow you to do that. Someone demands that you not love a person of another race or colour? I am sorry. This is 'Zero' and the Tai Chi person cannot yield. Someone wants you to support religious hatred? I am sorry. This is 'Zero' and the Tai Chi person must resist.

In the world of ego, the Tai Chi person flows around the mountains of anger in his path. In the world of our real nature, the world of Tai Chi, the world must flow around the Tai Chi person. Thus, Tai Chi is called,

'The Unmoving Movement'. In the world of ego, Tai Chi people are continuously moving but in the world of their nature, they are perfectly still and unchanging from their rootedness in the love that is their Wu Chi nature.

Chapter 13

Microcosm – Macrocosm

The Tao is forever undefined.
Small though it is in the unformed
state, it cannot be grasped.
If kings and lords could harness it,
The ten thousand things would
naturally obey.
Heaven and earth would come together
And gentle rain fall.

VERSE 32

L ove is the Tai Chi answer to all problems encountered in life, whether it is a problem between individual human beings (the microcosm) or a world problem (the macrocosm). I know that it seems boring to hear the same answer to every problem. Lao Tzu writes,

Passers-by may stop for music and good food,
But a description of the Tao
Seems without substance or flavour.

Verse 35

Nevertheless, the Tai Chi answer is reality. Anger, resistance, vengeance, screaming, marching, making wars are all far more exciting but they answer nothing. Tai Chi puts the burden of harmony on the individual loving heart. If there is a problem, it is the Tai Chi person's fault because it means that he or she did not love enough. All the principles upon which the great Tao operates – love, non-violence, compassion, humility – are also the principles upon which the individual must operate.

☯ The Yin of Tai Chi

The same rules apply for the behaviour of nations and individuals.

One of my Tai Chi students came to me once to tell me about a problem she was having with her mother. My student is 30 years old, unmarried and lives alone in a small apartment in town. Her mother is always calling her to ask her what she is doing, where she is going and who she is seeing. My student was developing a very strong resentment and dislike for her mother because of this constant checking-up on her behaviour. She asked me what the Tai Chi answer was to her problem. Of course, the answer is love. My student has not convinced her mother that she loves her.

The mother has a need to know that her only daughter at the age of 30 still loves her. She has an ego and cannot simply ask her daughter. The mother is afraid to reveal her need. If I tell you that I love you and that I need your love, I give you power to hurt me. If I ask you if you love me, you will know of my need and can hurt me whenever you feel like it by denying me expressions of your love. As long as you do not know of my need for your love, you can still hurt me but not on purpose.

To tell you of my need is to lower the walls I have built around myself to keep pain and suffering out.

The mother cannot ask and so she takes out her frustration by prying into her daughter's life. When she calls her daughter and asks her 'What have you been doing today?' what she is really asking is 'Do you love me?' Her heart is crying out in anguish to know it is loved by the one it loves so much. People want to be loved because loving and being loved is our Wu Chi nature. Seeing nothing lovable in our ego-centred selves, we seek wealth, fame, power, status, and such like, hoping that these will draw love to us.

The Tai Chi person's life is an answering of this need for love in others. We are the Wu Chi's love flowing to her children. With my Tai Chi student, her problem with her mother was her fault. She has not made her mother aware of her love for her. She must take every opportunity to show her. Once the mother is convinced of her daughter's love, the problem will end.

I learned this lesson from *my* mother. When I was 30, I had just finished my masters degree and was planning a trip around the world to visit the spiritual centres of the world's religions. My travels would take me through some dangerous places including Afghanistan, Iran and Israel. The night before I left, my mother accused me of doing something very bad. I could not believe it. I had not done what I was accused of and now here I was the night before my departure for a two-year journey in a heated argument with my mother.

Then, it dawned on me. My mother loved me very much and she was going to miss me, plus she was afraid for me. But she could not come out and say, 'John, I love you very much and I wish you would not go.' So, instead, she wanted to hurt me. If I could be hurt by her, it would demonstrate that I loved her because only those whom we love can hurt us. Therefore, on my journey, I wrote regularly to her of my love for her.

By humbling ourselves before the anger of others and by allowing our love to flow freely, Tai Chi people overcome the problem in their path. What is true for the microcosm is also true for the macrocosm. To solve international problems, nations must root themselves in humility and allow their love for the citizens of other nations to flow forth.

The Kosovo conflict in Eastern Europe would never have occurred if the advice of Lao Tzu had been heeded. Milosevic and Serbia had a problem. One of their provinces, which contained the most sacred site of Serbian history, was populated by people of a different religion who felt disaffected from the nation and oppressed by the Serbian population and government. Milosevic's answer to this problem was to seek the depopulation of the province. But, as Lao Tzu writes,

> Whenever you advise a ruler in the way of Tao,
> Counsel him not to use force to conquer the
> universe.
> For this would only cause resistance.
>
> Verse 30

This was exactly what occurred in Kosovo. With the Serbian effort forcibly to suppress Kosovo, the Albanian population began an armed resistance.

Lao Tzu further writes,

> What others teach, I also teach; that is
> A violent man will die a violent death.
> This will be the essence of my teaching.
>
> Verse 42

The use of force by Milosevic violated the principles of Tao and to violate the principles upon which the universe operates is to invite catastrophe. How could Milosevic and the Serbians have solved their problem in harmony with the principles of Tao? Lao Tzu gives the answer when he writes,

> A great country is like low land.
> It is the meeting ground of the universe,
> The mother of the universe.
> The female overcomes the male with stillness,

Lying low in stillness.
Therefore if a great country gives way to a
     smaller country,
It will conquer the smaller country.
And if a small country submits to a great
     country,
It can conquer the great country.
Therefore those who would conquer must yield,
And those who conquer do so because they yield.

Verse 61

The Serbians need the loyalty of Kosovo in order to protect their sacred site and to be united in their efforts to make a better life for the people of Serbia. Kosovo needs the economic strength of Serbia to help overcome its poverty and the Kosovars need to feel a part of the national society, and that their religion and culture are respected. So, unification would be advantageous to both the Serbians and the Kosovars. It is only the means that Milosevic used in seeking to accomplish this unification that violated the Tao.

Milosevic chose to play the role of the aggressive male using force and thus creating catastrophe. Instead, Serbia should have played the role of the female. By 'lying low, in stillness' (that is, being humble), giving way to the small province of Kosovo, Serbia could have united with the Albanians peacefully, with joy on both sides. Milosevic could have spoken to the Albanians, telling them that the Serbians understood their fears of Serbian domination. Then he could have invited the Albanians to draw up whatever laws and provisions the Albanians felt necessary to protect their rights and culture, and that would make them feel that they, too, were a part of this great effort at nation building.

The Albanians, expressing their understanding of Serbian fears and dreams, could have agreed. Then, voices and dreams would have power. The Albanians would no longer feel like second-class citizens. Their energies, hopes and desires would be channelled into the Serbian effort of nation building. And this result might have shown the way to solving

Indonesia's problem with the province of Aceh, India's problem with Kashmir, Turkey's problem with the Kurds, and so on.

Serbian yielding to the Albanians of Kosovo could have thus been the beginning of a new age, a lesson to all peoples of how humility, yieldingness and compassion for the welfare of a country's citizens can overcome centuries of separation and conflict. Milosevic would have taken his place as one of the world's great heroes. But, instead of this Taoistic path, Milosevic decided to attack. Why? Because of ego. Milosevic wanted to be the ruler and as Lao Tzu writes, there is

**No greater misfortune than wanting something
for oneself.**

Verse 46

Milosevic did not follow the Tao and the way of love. Thus,

When the Tao is present in the universe,

The horses haul manure.
When the Tao is absent from the universe,
War horses are bred outside the city.

Verse 46

My student who had the problem with her mother chose the way of Tai Chi – humility, yieldingness and compassion. As a result, she has destroyed the ego's walls that surrounded her mother and a harmonious relationship rooted in love and oneness now exists between them. Milosevic rejected the way of Tai Chi, choosing rather to follow the way of ambition and force, and he brought disharmony, war, death and destruction.

Whether in the microcosm or the macrocosm, the principles remain the same. Until the nations accept the way of compassionate love, human history will remain a history of hatred and war. Nations will remain in the realm of ego based upon force, ambition, separation and competition until each of us individual human beings turns toward the love that lies within our Wu Chi nature.

Chapter 14

The Tai Chi School

The wise student hears of the Tao and practises it diligently.

VERSE 41

In the pursuit of learning, every day something is acquired.
In the pursuit of Tao, every day something is dropped.

VERSE 48

Tai Chi is Wu Chi expressing itself in reality; potential love becoming real love. Thus, Tai Chi is reality. You are doing Tai Chi when you open your heart and allow the love of your Wu Chi nature to flow outward to touch upon others. By doing this, you reveal yourself to the universe and thus become real. By loving, you move from Wu Chi to Tai Chi.

This movement from potential love to real love *is* Tai Chi. Hence, it is easy to see that in order to do Tai Chi, you do not need a Tai Chi school, a Tai Chi teacher or Tai Chi movements. There are many Tai Chi people in the world who have never heard of Tai Chi. They are loving Christians or loving Moslems or loving Buddhists or loving atheists, and so on. The Tai Chi school, Tai Chi teacher and Tai Chi movements are merely aids to help you learn to live a life of Tai Chi more quickly. They are not absolutely necessary for a journey to the Tao.

The form of Tai Chi I teach, The Sun-Moon Circle Northern Shao-lin Yang Style Tai Chi, is very extended, requiring a great deal of flexibility and balance. In each class, before we begin the Tai Chi movements, we make a circle and do a series of warming-up exercises designed to improve the student's balance, flexibility, lung capacity and concentration. These warming-up exercises are not necessary in order to do the Tai Chi movements. The movements themselves will give the student these physical abilities. The warming-up exercises only make the process work more quickly.

Like the warming-up exercises, the Tai Chi school, the Tai Chi teacher and the Tai Chi movements are designed merely to quicken the process whereby the students root themselves in their Wu Chi nature, allowing their love to flow to all things.

All of Tai Chi is imitation and example. The Tai Chi person imitates the Tao and its flowing from Non-Being into Being; from Wu Chi into Tai Chi. Thus, the Tai Chi school is an imitation of the Tao, also. It is an island of tranquillity, harmony, silence and peace in the midst of the world of the ego that surrounds it. Within its walls, the world of ego disappears and the old Mother World lives again.

The Tai Chi school is the garden of the Jian. Everything within it has meaning and uniqueness. It is a place of emptiness, a part of the Void surrounded by walls. It is the Wu Chi. Like the Zen garden, there is very little in it. When the students step through the door, they enter into the emptiness that is their inner nature, where everything is clear and pure. Anger, envy, jealousy, troubles from the outer world, pain – all fade away as the students slip into the Void of the Tai Chi school.

Like the Jian gardener, the Tai Chi teacher arranges every object in the school – pictures, plants, chairs, lights, and so on – so that the uniqueness of their nature adds to the harmony and tranquillity of the whole. This is a process that takes many years, as a plant is moved here or a painting moved there. The Tai Chi teacher becomes the Jian, helping everything to find its place in the oneness, helping everything's spirit to find that special place where it finds its fulfilment in the whole.

In this atmosphere, students glide effortlessly into their own special place in the circle of other students that is the Tai Chi school, finding where their spirit can flower in all its glory, adding to the beauty of the whole. The Tai Chi school is a miniature Tao where people, plants and inanimate objects merge together in love and harmony, demonstrating to the students how the world outside the school should be so that the students can become the gardeners of their own lives.

The Tai Chi school is a place of silence. There is no loud music, traffic noises, arguments, and such like, but only the silence of the Void. In silence, the rational mind has nothing to focus upon and thus turns inward and moves towards the inner nature, the true reality of the individual. It is this silence that is so feared and shunned in the world of ego outside the door. People do not want to see what lies within because then they would see the meaninglessness of their lives. Thus, people feel uneasy in moments of silence when no one is talking or the radio is off. But, in the Tai Chi school, it is exactly this knowledge of the inner self that we are seeking and silence eases our way inward. Then the students will see that their inner being is

Something mysteriously formed,
Born before heaven and earth.
In the silence and the void. . .

Verse 25

In the Tai Chi school, the students return to the womb of all creation. All of the things that make the world of ego what it is disappear within the walls of the Tai Chi school. Hence, the students can escape the hard coldness, pain, ambition, aggression and competition that drive the world of ego, and return to the warm loving womb of the Wu Chi. In the Tai Chi school, there are no ranks, no trophies to win, no place for competition and ambition. All separating labels disappear. Opinions about the fictional world of the ego are left outside the door. Labels such as businessman, lawyer, housewife, college student, conservative, liberal, Christian, Jew, American, European, rich, poor, white, brown, and such like have no meaning. There are only human beings who need to love and be loved.

In the Tai Chi school, the students escape the storms of life and can open their hearts, seeking oneness with themselves and oneness with each other. The Tai Chi school is a group of people who have come together in order to recreate the loving universe that existed before the rational mind destroyed it. The students become the doorway through which the love of the Wu Chi can enter reality and thus the Tai Chi students help in the creating of themselves and the creating of the universe.

We all have negative places within ourselves which we have to rid ourselves of in order to flow with the love that is our nature. In our efforts to rid ourselves of these negativities, we hurt those whom we love. If you love me, it will hurt you when you see me do something low and base. The more you love me, the more I will hurt with my unloving actions. I am sure in my own life, I have hurt my wife more than anyone else ever has because she loves me so much. Her love makes her see the beauty of my soul and when I do something that keeps others from seeing that beauty, it hurts her. Seeing her pain causes me to look at myself and my actions. Because of her love for me and my love for her, her pain forces me to become a better person. Thus, the person that I love the most, I have hurt the most.

And yet, she continues to love me. She offers herself to me and opens her heart to me so that I have a place in which to work out the negative aspects of myself. That is the nature of love. If you do not love me and I do something bad to you, you will leave me. But, if you really love me, you will remain with me, using your love to help me find the way. Because you love me, I must listen to you. If you do not love me and I do something unloving, then what do I care what you think? Who are you that I should listen to you? But, if you love me and I see that I have caused you pain, it hurts me also, and I must examine my behaviour. Your love becomes my guide and teacher.

Just so, the Tai Chi school is a group of people who have come together to seek oneness with themselves and the universe, opening their hearts to each other in an effort to provide each other with a testing ground for the Tai Chi principles of humility, cooperation and compassion. The other students become your 'friends' who will allow you to experiment with them in your effort to lead a loving life.

The destiny of Tai Chi people is to travel through the world of ego using their love to pierce the walls of the egos that surround people, touching them with love of the Wu Chi and thus making them and the world live again. This process of reaching out with love, feeling around the walls of others, gently probing until your love finds that special place where it can flow inward to the true self of the other is learned by practising upon the other students in the Tai Chi school.

I have seen this love between students develop in the Tai Chi classes so much that if one student is missing, there is an emptiness, a missing piece in the harmony of the group. This is the greatest pleasure for a Tai Chi teacher, to see this oneness, this compassion and caring develop, for then he knows that his school is truly a 'place of the Way'.

Another aspect of the Tai Chi school is to serve as the 'mirror of the universe'. Mirrors do not lie. You look in a mirror and see things as they really are. Outside the school, in the world of ego, the students are assaulted continuously by anger, arrogance, insensitivity, and such like. When they make a mistake, they are yelled at and abused. If I bump into someone, I am yelled at. If I make a mistake while driving my car, people honk at me and swear.

People judge me by their hard, fixed ideas of the way the world should be and attach labels to me. They put me in categories and then treat me as they have defined me – good or bad, conservative or liberal, and so on. I am treated as a dead plastic thing. I am a vent for their frustration and anger, a stepping stone for their ambitions.

In such a world, it is easy to forget who I really am, to forget the beauty and glory that are my soul. I begin to feel that the constant pointing out of my faults and the anger directed toward me, the lack of love, compassion and understanding that are shown to me are, in fact, deserved because I am unworthy. Plus, as someone seeking to realize my true loving nature, I am highly sensitive to my faults and failures. They are always before me and always being emphasized by the world around me. If someone drives by a muddy puddle and splashes water on a man in the world of ego, he will yell at the driver in anger and feel righteous in doing so. If I am splashed and get angry and yell at the driver, it hurts my soul because I know this is not the Way. At such times, it is hard for me to remember the beauty of who I am.

But, when I step through the door of the Tai Chi school and feel its peace and tranquillity, when I see the love and friendship offered me, then I remember who and what I am. I see the beauty of my spirit reflected in the eyes of the other members of the school. They are a mirror in which I see the love of my own Wu Chi nature in all its purity, untouched by the anger and judgement of others or by my own petty failures.

Once, I received a letter from a young man I met on a Kibbutz in Israel where we were both studying Hebrew. I really liked him and we became good friends. He was so ready to smile, so gentle with himself and other people that it was impossible not to love him. We had long discussions about spiritual development, Tai Chi, meditation, and such like. When we returned to the USA, he began to study Tai Chi and worked with Zen Buddhism.

With the beginning of a spiritual journey, we begin to turn inward and when we do, we see all of our pettiness, the dark negative spots on our inner self. And, as I have said, the people around us reinforce this view of ourselves. They rub our noses in our failings, so much so that we forget that we are in fact engaging in the hardest struggle that human beings can engage in, the struggle to become real loving human beings. Thus, we only see our failings. This happened to my friend and in his letter to me he described how he seemed to be more aggressive and unloving. This depressed him greatly.

In my reply to him, I did not try to deny that he had those negative places or tell him not to worry about it, and so on. Instead, I tried to hold up a mirror to him. I ignored the negativities he spoke of and simply told him how beautiful a person he was and that his perseverance on his spiritual journey touched me deeply. I told him of the impact his warmth, compassion and friendliness had had upon me and how it had moved my heart to love him. I told him how glad I was to have him in my life, that our paths had crossed. In other words, I tried to use my words as a mirror so that by reading my letter he could see the beauty of his own Wu Chi nature which is who he really is. I hoped that my letter would remind him of who he truly was and what glory and beauty awaited him. Sometime later, my friend visited me and told me how much my letter had helped him overcome his depression.

The Tai Chi school serves the same function as my letter to my friend. When a student enters wounded in spirit from the harshness of the world outside, the teacher and the other students remind the student of how valiant and full of glory his or her efforts to bring love to the universe are. They remind the student of the ocean of love that is the student's home and of the mercy and compassion that are flowing from the student's nature in an effort to ease the pain and suffering of the world.

The Tai Chi school is the mirror. Look in and you will see within yourself the love and the compassion of the Mother Tao. You will see the beauty of your own soul which the world of ego tries to make you lose sight of.

Chapter 15

The Tai Chi Movements

The great Tao flows…

Verse 34

Water gives life to the Ten Thousand
Things and does not strive.
It flows in places men reject and so is like
The Tao.

Verse 8

Soft and weak overcome hard and strong.

Verse 36

The greatest mistake that Tai Chi students can make is believing that coming to the Tai Chi school and learning the Tai Chi movements is the essence of Tai Chi. Learning to open your heart and allowing the love of your Wu Chi nature to flow outward to touch upon the world is Tai Chi. To identify Tai Chi with the movements is to lose the meaning of Tai Chi and reduce it to sport. The Tai Chi movements are merely aids in helping practitioners to root themselves in their Wu Chi nature so that Tai Chi can become possible.

Thus, it always bothers me as a teacher when a student thinks they are not a good Tai Chi person because they cannot do the movements very well. If I just wanted pretty movements, I would only take dancers into my school. There is no way to judge if a student is 'good' or 'bad' in Tai Chi. Tai Chi occurs inside the student.

In Karate classes, the students all bow to the master first and then the master bows to the students in return. The students bow first in acknowledgement of the master's superior position in having done Karate for a much longer time than the students. But in Tai Chi, students and teacher bow to everyone else at the same time because none knows who has done Tai Chi the longest. The teacher has done the movements the longest but the movements are unimportant. Who has done Tai Chi the longest? Maybe you are a student who just joined the school today for your first Tai Chi lesson and I have been doing the Tai Chi movements for 30 years but it could be that you are already much closer to living in accordance with the Tao than I am.

However, the movements are an aid in realizing a life of Tai Chi and they are specifically designed to that end. The first step in doing the Tai Chi movements, as in living a Tai Chi life, is to find our Wu Chi nature and to become rooted in it. Without the Wu Chi, Tai Chi is impossible.

Before the Tao existed, before anything was, there was only Wu Chi

The Wu Chi moved and created Tai Chi; Reality

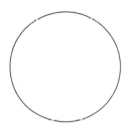

The combination of Wu Chi and Tai Chi, and the movement of Wu Chi to Tai Chi and back to Wu Chi again in a continuous, eternal process, is the Tao, or Way.

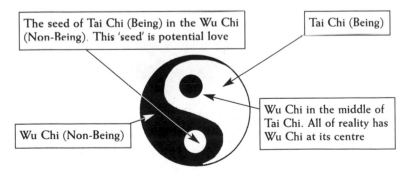

The seed of Tai Chi (Being) in the Wu Chi (Non-Being). This 'seed' is potential love

Tai Chi (Being)

Wu Chi (Non-Being)

Wu Chi in the middle of Tai Chi. All of reality has Wu Chi at its centre

Within Wu Chi (Non-Being) lies the possibility of Tai Chi (Being). Potential love is the 'seed' from which Tai Chi can grow. The Wu Chi moves (expresses its love) and the seed grows into reality; the pregnant Wu Chi mother gives birth to the Tai Chi child. The universe that is created comes from the Wu Chi and the Wu Chi is its centre, its essence. Everything that exists is reality formed around Wu Chi. Wu Chi preceded Tai Chi. Without Wu Chi, there could have been no Tai Chi.

The person in the world of Ego is represented by

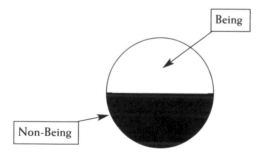

Here, the Wu Chi and Tai Chi are completely separated with Being unaware of Non-Being. The seed in Wu Chi is missing because there is no possibility of the Wu Chi being able to express its love in reality. The person is unaware of the potential love that is his Wu Chi nature. And, there is no Wu Chi at the centre of Being because the person is out of touch with the Wu Chi. Hence, there is no movement and the Tao is lost. There is only the stagnation that one sees in bodies of water that have no flow and thus have no possibility of true life.

What does all this mean for the Tai Chi person? It means that before students can attempt to do Tai Chi, they must first find their true nature, the Wu Chi. Without finding the Wu Chi at the centre of their being and becoming rooted in it, Tai Chi will not be possible. Wu Chi is the potential love that is their nature and Tai Chi is the expressing of that potential love in reality.

The first step of finding and becoming rooted in our Wu Chi nature is the taming of the rational mind. It is the rational mind that has separated us from our nature by usurping the role of guide through life.

Tai Chi tames the mind by focusing it in the 'Tan Tien'. What separates Oriental movements from Western physical exercises is that in the West we think that we can teach the body in separation from the spirit and mind. Hence, the mind is allowed to wander and the person doing push-ups can be thinking about the party on Saturday night. What their body is learning is only for the body and offers no lessons for their life or about their inner nature, who they really are. Hence, you can have great gymnasts who are very egotistical, dancers who cannot find peace in their private lives, and so on.

When the mind is in the Tan Tien, whatever I teach the body is also a lesson learned by the mind and spirit. The Tai Chi teaches the totality of the student. Tai Chi is the way of what is natural. It is our nature to love and the Tai Chi movements help us to follow this natural way by making us one with ourselves. All of the movements came from the observation of the movements of Nature – animals, bamboo in the wind, water flowing, and such like. It is from Nature that the principles of the Tai Chi movements are taken – flexibility, softness, balance, yieldingness and continuous movement.

In Tai Chi, when I teach the body flexibility, I also teach the spirit and mind to be flexible. Flexibility is freedom. The more flexible my body is the more physical movements I can make. Where before I could not work in the garden because my knees and back were not flexible, now I can. The more flexible my mind is the more ideas I can contemplate. Where before fixed, hard, set ideas kept me from accepting you as a friend because you held ideas that challenged or frightened me, now I have the flexibility to listen and my fear of you and your thinking disappears, allowing you to come close to me. The more flexible my spirit is the more I can feel and love. Where before I rejected you because you were of another religion or race, now my spirit is flexible enough to yield and let you in. Hence, flexibility is an essential if one is to be truly and fully alive.

Thus, Lao Tzu writes,

A man is born gentle and weak.
At his death he is hard and stiff.
Green plants are tender and filled with sap.

At their death they are withered and dry.
Therefore the stiff and unbending is the
        discipline of death.
The gentle and yielding is the discipline of
        life.

Verse 76

When the Tai Chi movements teach the body balance, they simultaneously teach the mind and the spirit balance. In Tai Chi self-defence, the Tai Chi person takes the aggressor's balance away and never allows him to get it back. The point is that if you are not balanced and in control of yourself, someone else will take control of your body and do whatever they wish with you and you will be defenceless.

The same is true for the mind. If you cannot control the fears that reside in your mind, someone else can use those fears to control you because your mind lacks balance. The balanced mind has no fear. Because it is not swayed, it sees clearly the state of things and the consequences of its reasoning and it is united with the heart which ensures that the mind's reasoning will flow from compassion. No matter what reason another person gives, your mind will not be swayed from its clear-sightedness.

If the spirit does not have balance and thus is easily moved from love to hate, someone else will control who you love and hate. Hence, Milosevic could move the Serbians to hate. Northern Ireland is another example of this ability of fanatical leaders to sway the spirits of their followers toward communal hatred.

The 108 movements of the Tai Chi Chuan are a story. From the first movement to the last, this story describes the creation of the universe, the arising of individual objects and their ultimate return to the Void. In the religious music of Hinduism, there is an instrument called a drone that plays a single note. This note never varies but continues from the beginning to the end of the 'Raga', or sacred song, never stopping. This instrument is joined by the sitar which plays various melodies, sometimes fast and sometimes slow.

This music is a description of the 'sacred' universe. The instrument

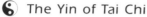

that makes the single note is the background upon which everything else occurs. This is the Om, the Sacred. This unwavering Om sound is the unmoving, unchanging sacredness that runs through all things and all time. It is the centre and essence of all things. It is true reality. The dancing notes of the sitar are the everyday occurrences of our lives. The music is saying that as we move through the varying activities of our lives, we should remember and remain rooted in the eternal, sacred centre that is the essence of all things.

Tai Chi students are also 'playing' the sacred song of the universe. They are giving a concert using their bodies as the instruments. The students' Wu Chi nature to which they unwaveringly adhere is the Om sound of the drone and their bodies describe the various, ever-changing conditions of life. But as they continuously move, they remain rooted in the love of their Wu Chi nature. Thus, the body is their instrument through which they play the song of creation and reality, and the Tai Chi movements are the notes of that loving melody.

When students are about to begin the Tai Chi Chuan, they sink their minds into Tan Tien and relax their bodies, settling themselves into the harmony, peace and tranquillity at their centre, reaching for the Wu Chi. When the Wu Chi is attained and they are rooted in love and calmness, they remain motionless, waiting. They are in the Wu Chi. They are Non-Being. They are in the position they were in before their emergence from the Void at birth. They are Nothingness, No-Thing, waiting for the Wu Chi to express its love in reality.

Slowly, a moving force begins at their centre, flowing through them until the body begins to move as the left foot overcomes the inertia of Non Being and spontaneously, without their conscious volition, begins to slide into the Tai Chi stance. At this exact second when the foot begins to move spontaneously, the movement from Non-Being into Being has begun. Love pours forth from the students' Wu Chi nature to express itself in the movements; Tai Chi has begun. Thus, this first movement re-enacts the creation of the universe when the Wu Chi spontaneously flowed into reality. But, it is more then an enactment. It is also a participation in that creation because the Wu Chi is continuously creating the universe and the students' Wu Chi nature is part of this creative process.

This first move is the birth of the individual from the womb of Wu Chi. There is a sense of excitement and awe as when a father watches the tip of the baby's head emerge from the mother's body. It is as if the whole universe is watching and waiting, holding its breath to see what new wonder will appear from the Wu Chi, what new mystery will unfold. And as the student's foot begins to move, it is like the baby's head emerging and there is a feeling that there is a great celebration throughout the Tao; stars sing, the rivers laugh, leaves whisper to each other at the stupendous glory that is being revealed. The Wu Chi has moved. The cherry blossom has bloomed.

As the movements progress, flowing from one into the next without pause, the life of the individual is described with its soaring highs, diving lows and continuous twisting, turning and yielding. The fluidity and beauty of the moves reveal the individual's existence in all its glory, moving the hearts of all who see it so that it is not only the student who is filled with tranquillity and peace but also all who watch him or her move.

For this procession of movements to be real Tai Chi, the students must do them with their soul. They must open themselves completely in order to feel every atom of their being, to experience all the myriad aspects of their nature acting upon the universe. There is a danger that doing the movements will become routine. A student may show up at class tired and just move their body through the form. But this is not Tai Chi. It is only when the student's soul is involved in the movements for all the world to see that Tai Chi is occurring.

Everyone will experience the movements differently because everyone has their own unique nature. When I do 'White Crane Spread Wings', the right arm rises high above the head, the body is stretched upward to its fullest height, the torso is twisted. This gives me the feeling of the agony and suffering and pain of life – of starving people, of a mother who has lost her child, of a war that takes young men's lives, of people broken in despair and loneliness. But also as I stretch upward there is a tremendous hope that I can somehow rid the world of such pain and heartbreak.

Then, the body comes flowing downward to the earth in total, dark, absolute, soul-crushing despair for I know that there is nothing I can do. Once again, the body rises as the left arm soars above the head, seeking again to lift the tired world from its knees as it is crushed under the burden of suffering, but this time I do not soar quite as high and inevitably when my body must once more bow toward the earth, the hopelessness and despair return. But this time the despair is not so overwhelming because I already knew before I began that there was no hope. At the conclusion of the move, I rise again to my full height with my arms spread wide and high embracing all of reality, showing the world the Tai Chi life in all its glory and splendour.

Finally, the students near the end of the movements. Movement 107 is 'Priest Shows Respect to the People'. In this move, life is almost done. The cherry blossom hangs on the tree by a mere thread. The students bow to the universe, accepting things as they are – life and death, pain and joy.

The last movement is death, the return to the oneness of the Void, the return to the womb of the Wu Chi as the students return to the original, motionless state in which the movements began. But there is no sadness because even in the stillness, the tranquillity and peace of the Wu Chi is rooted in their hearts. When the students are finished and the movements have ceased, there yet remains a faint memory of the beauty that was, a memory that those who watched will take with them as they disperse to go back to their busy lives.

The greatest danger for the Tai Chi journeyer is to mistake what happens inside the Tai Chi school as Tai Chi. This is a critical point for the Tai Chi student to grasp – the school is only a temporary refuge from the storm of life in the world of ego. It is not the hermit's cave of a monastery, but only a wayside inn. It is not a place to hide.

As the students go through their daily life, they are continuously pressured, pushed, hurt and slammed around by the hardness and unlovingness in the world of ego. Their heart is ever being cast against the hard walls the ego constructs around the hearts of others. Then, for a short while, they can escape into the warmth, peace and tranquillity of the Tai Chi school where there are others who are seeking to love the universe. Here, in the school, they can learn and practise the principles of a loving life. But then the Tai Chi students must leave this small world of the loving Wu Chi mother and go back out into the storm.

The Tai Chi school is only a place for renewing energy and practising for life. If the lessons learned in the movements are not used in our lives outside the school, the Tai Chi school has no meaning. The students do not 'do' Tai Chi in the Tai Chi school but only practise. Tai Chi is done in the world of ego. Thus, the students must not get into the habit of thinking that they do Tai Chi on Thursday nights from 6 to 8 o'clock, and when class is over they can forget about Tai Chi until next Thursday. Without the practising in the outside world of the lessons learned in the Tai Chi school, Tai Chi becomes merely a pastime, a sport, an amusement. Rather than taking the love of the Wu Chi out into the world, the students would be bringing the deadening and meaningless influence of the world of ego into the Tai Chi school.

The vast majority of the students' Tai Chi lessons will come not from the school and the movements, but from outside. Everything and everyone is our Tai Chi teacher. All we have to do is to be aware of this fact. Everything we encounter and everyone we meet has something to teach us if we are but sensitive enough to learn. This, of course, requires an awareness that Tai Chi is an every-second-of-your-life thing and not confined to your two hours a week in the Tai Chi school.

For example, one day last summer I was cutting grass in my chicken yard in order to make hay for my sheep. It was very hot. There is a beehive by the gate of the chicken yard and the bees become very aggressive in hot, humid weather. As I was swinging my scythe, I saw a bee coming directly toward me. And then, after 31 years of practising Tai Chi, I forgot the first lesson Tai Chi teaches – do not resist aggression. If I had remained still and quiet, the bee would have gone away, having found no target for its aggression. Instead, I hit at it, trying to make it go away. Needless to say, this enraged it even more and it stung me on the head. I assure you, the bee taught me a Tai Chi lesson that I will remember for a long time.

If I had not realized that Tai Chi is everyday life, I would just have been a man cutting grass who was stung by a bee. The bee, the grass and I would have existed in separation from each other with no lesson learned but to stay away from bees. But, because of my awareness of what Tai Chi truly is, the bee, the grass and I were doing Tai Chi. The bee taught me a lesson not just about bees, but about life and the universe. What I learned from the bee I can use in every aspect of my life. Hence, the universe was doing Tai Chi with me. And thus, I am very thankful to that bee, although I hope there are not too many such lessons from his kind.

With this understanding of Tai Chi, all of life becomes a Tai Chi lesson, the universe becomes the Tai Chi school and everything you do becomes a Tai Chi movement. Anyone who confines Tai Chi to the inside of the Tai Chi school loses an infinite opportunity to learn and thus live a life of Tai Chi.

Chapter 16

The Tai Chi Teacher

The Tao that can be told is not the eternal Tao.

VERSE 1

L ao Tzu writes,

> Those who know do not talk.
> Those who talk do not know.
>> **Verse 56**

and,

> In the beginning those who knew the Tao did
>> not try to enlighten others. . .
>>> **Verse 65**

What Lao Tzu is saying is that once the Tai Chi journeyer has rooted him- or herself in their Wu Chi nature and re-established their oneness with the Tao, they disappear into the oneness, passing through life unnoticed. Their life is their teaching. What they 'know' cannot be taught, so there is no sense in trying to 'enlighten' others. Tai Chi is something that occurs within the student. How can such internal processes be taught? What this means is that the Tai Chi teacher does not know the way back to the Tao. If he did, he would not be teaching. How can you teach that which is beyond teaching? Hence, the Tai Chi teacher does not have the position of honour that is accorded to other teachers in the Oriental disciplines.

The Zen Master, the Guru, the Tea Master, the Karate Master – all know the path to where they are going. They deserve to be honoured for what they know and for their ability to take the students by the hand and lead them to the goal. By contrast, the Tai Chi teacher is merely someone stumbling around in the dark, searching for some unknown something and with no idea of how to get there. That is why there is no such thing as a 'great' Tai Chi teacher.

Thus, when I say that I have been on the Tai Chi journey for 31 years, that is not bragging but rather a confession. In 31 years I have not been able to find the elusive oneness with the Tao that is the driving force of my life. My Tai Chi teaching and my writing of Tai Chi books are the proofs of my failure. In our system of Tai Chi, after 10 years you are a 'priest' and after 30 years a 'master'. But, these are not titles of honour or respect, merely statements that the journeyer has been seeking the Tao for 10 or 30 years and has still not succeeded.

So, why do people become Tai Chi teachers? All I can do to answer this question is to describe my own journey. Since I first discovered *The Tao Te Ching* and the teachings of Lao Tzu, I have been haunted by the vision of the Mother Tao. Wherever I turned in life, I saw her face before me 'dimly seen as through a veil'. I was awed by the vision of warmth and love her eyes offered me and I spent my years chasing after her.

But, the Mother is ever elusive, always just beyond reach. Sometimes, I would be so close to her that I could hear her cosmic breath, and at other times I felt so far away that she seemed like only a distant dream. I would see her out of the corner of my eye, hiding behind a tree, and I would race over just to see her disappearing around the next corner of the path. Again I would race ahead only to hear her laughter floating on the wind somewhere down the path behind me.

Sometimes I could not stand the terrible yearning and frustration any more and I would seek to ignore the Mother Tao, but at night when I slept she would come to me and whisper to my soul. So, I went on and on, day after day, year after year seeking she who is my essence, who is my Wu Chi nature.

After I left my master's school to become a wandering Taoist, I was truly alone with no one with whom I could share my visions of the Mother Tao, no one to turn to for comfort when overcome by my constant failure to reach the level of love that would allow me at last to take my place in the oneness of the Tao. I felt strange and outcast, a failure in life. I would see the young men around me who would seem to know exactly where they were going in life and exactly what they were going to do. They has gold wristwatches, sports cars and beautiful girlfriends. Society approved of them and all doors were open to them while I wandered aimlessly, looking for magic and mystery. Thus, Verse 20 of *The Tao Te Ching* is the verse that touches my heart and soul more than any other:

Other people are contented, enjoying the
      sacrificial feast of the ox.
In spring some go to the park, and climb
      the terrace
But I alone am drifting, not knowing where
      I am,
Like a newborn babe before it learns to
      smile,
I am alone, without a place to go.

Others have more then they need, but I
      alone have nothing.
I am a fool. Oh, yes. I am confused.
Other men are clear and bright,
But I alone am dim and weak.
Other men are sharp and clever,
But I alone am dull and stupid.

Oh, I drift like the waves of the sea,
Without direction, like the restless wind.

Everyone else is busy,
But I alone am aimless and depressed.
I am different.
I am nourished by the great mother.

After years of this 'aloneness' aspect of the Tai Chi journey, I decided to open my own Tai Chi school. My hope was to be with others who also felt the yearning of their Wu Chi natures, others who felt all alone in the cold, hard world of the ego and were seeking to return to the loving world of the Mother Tao. With a school, I would be able to see the love of the Tao shining out through the eyes of my students. I would not be alone any more.

A special bond is formed when the teacher and the students join together to form a Tai Chi school. Lao Tzu writes,

If the teacher is not respected,
And the student is not cared for,
Confusion will arise, however clever one is.

Verse 27

What Lao Tzu is saying is that when the teacher accepts a student, he must be willing to 'care for' (that is love) that student. He must feel a compassion for the student's yearning to become one with themselves which mirrors the teacher's own yearning. He must become one with their dreams and hopes of peace and tranquillity. He must constantly throw his heart against them until his love is allowed in, so that joining of the teacher and students in oneness can occur.

Like Jacob and the Angel, the teacher must wrestle with the souls of his students until he receives their blessing, which is their allowing his love to enter. In so doing, he teaches by example how the Tai Chi person flows through life in the world of ego. How could the teacher show the student the way of Tai Chi (love expressed in reality) if he did not love his students? The Tai Chi school cannot exist without this flow of love from the teacher toward the student.

For the students' part, they must respect the teacher. Not respect that the teacher knows where he is going or what he is doing, but rather that the teacher is really, seriously trying to find his way back to the oneness of the Tao. The student must believe that the teacher is focusing all the aspects of his life, all of his energy, and all of his being toward oneness with himself and the universe. Without this respect of the student for the teacher, the true Tai Chi school cannot exist and only movements can be taught.

The Tai Chi teacher teaches by example. He follows the advice of Lao Tzu,

Be an example to the world.
Verse 28

The teacher is an example, but not an example of the correct way to do things, for then he would be one with the Tao and would stop being a teacher. Rather, the teacher is an example of the mistakes that should be avoided. The teacher is constantly making mistakes as he seeks to find the right path back to the Tao. Thus, the Tai Chi teacher's life is what the Zen call 'Shoshaku jushaku' or 'One Continuous Mistake'.

What is happening in the Tai Chi school is that the teacher and the students are stumbling around, lost in the darkness that is the mystery of the Tao. The Tao is a mystery beyond rational understanding, so the teacher cannot know where he is going. The teacher leads in the sense that he is in front and the students are following behind. The students watch the teacher trip and stumble as he seeks to live a life of Tai Chi and they pass the word along to watch out for this mistake that the teacher has just made. Through the teacher's example of what not to do, they avoid the same mistakes. They do not trust that the teacher is taking them in the right direction but only that he will keep going until he finds what he is seeking, no matter how long it takes or how hard the going becomes. All this means that when the teacher fails to live up to the ideals of love and compassion in his daily life, he must give the students a description of his failure and explain how the mistake occurred.

Needless to say, I have made a tremendous number of mistakes on my journey and I am continually having to explain to my students my failings. Sometimes it is about how I got angry with my neighbour, or was not nice to my wife or a lesson I learned from a bee while cutting grass.

The Tai Chi life is a life of tiny victories, such as not getting mad at the person who cuts in front of you in line for the cinema, and overwhelming, crushing, grind-you-in-the-dirt defeats, such as not having loved the world enough to prevent the war in Kosovo, knowing that the deaths in Eastern Europe are your fault because you have not done that which you were supposed to do, and that is to bring the love of Wu Chi into the universe.

These tiny victories and huge defeats are the teachings of the Tai Chi teacher. After each crushing failure, the teacher must rise again to continue the journey and the effort to bring love, tranquillity, harmony and peace to the universe. And after each failure the teacher is a little more experienced and has a few more scars on his heart. This ability to continue is only possible because of the love the teacher has for his students, which is why Lao Tzu describes this love as essential. When the teacher looks into the faces of his students and sees their beauty, he knows that he must continue his lost stumbling around in the darkness of his ignorance seeking the bright path that will lead them all to their home in the Wu Chi.

The teacher is also a student. Just as everything in the universe is the teacher of the Tai Chi person, so every student is the teacher of the Tai Chi teacher. So much of what the teacher learns is the result of students relating a personal problem to him or asking him to explain certain aspects of Tai Chi. These things require the teacher to delve ever deeper into the meaning of Tai Chi. So, the Tai Chi school is a group of people teaching each other Tai Chi with one (the Tai Chi teacher) merely giving order to the class and school.

In fact, I have learned great lessons from my students. Tai Chi is concerned only with this second of your life. Do you have peace and tranquillity within you and are you existing in a loving, harmonious relationship with all things in this second? Lao Tzu does not tell us if there are gods, if there is a heaven or a hell, reincarnation, and such like. In two verses, he speaks of death:

> Being at one with the Tao is eternal.
> And though the body dies, the Tao will never
> pass away.
>
> Verse 16

and,

> To die but not perish is to be eternally
> present.
>
> Verse 33

But, what do these verses mean? We continue beyond death somehow, but how? Lao Tzu does not say.

One student especially burned her lesson into my soul. I have not spent much time thinking about what happens after death because this second of life is what is important. But then a student of mine died. I had never had a student die before, so this was a totally new experience. Her name was Barbara Schmid and she was 38 years old. She was very beautiful inside as well as outside. The teacher must love all of his students but some take longer to love than others. Barbara was a student I loved the second she stepped into my school. She had been with the school for seven years when she found out suddenly that she was dying and only had a short time to live.

Barbara had known of my love for her for a long time and when she heard the news, she asked me to come to her hospital room to see her. The news shocked me and her wish that I visit her frightened me. I had never dealt with a dying person before. What do you say to such a person? I had no idea and was very confused.

☯ The Yin of Tai Chi

Chuang Tzu tells the story of a Confucianist who was walking through the countryside when he came to a village from which he heard the sounds of music, dancing and laughter. He wondered what kind of celebration the people were having and entered the village gate. He saw a group of Taoists dancing, drinking and celebrating in the village square. He walked up to one of the Taoists and asked him the cause of the celebration. The Taoist responded, 'Our master has died. He has returned to the Great Void and is one with the Mother Tao.'

As I have said, I am not yet able to live up to the ideals expressed in Tai Chi philosophy. I could not live up to the example of these celebrating Taoists. Barbara's class was meeting that evening and so I went to the school before I went to see Barbara. The first student who arrived was a woman named Pia and I told her as soon as she walked in that I loved her very much. My students are used to this, so she just smiled in return. The class arrived and sat against the wall as I told them of Barbara. The entire time I was talking, images of the beauty, love and compassion Barbara had brought to our school kept flitting through my mind.

Then one of my students began to weep and that was it. I told Pia that I had told her of my love for her because we never know when that which we love will be taken from us and you must let people know that you love them right now so that your Wu Chi nature is expressed and your love is real. Then, I began to cry and could not go on, even as I tried to tell the other students of my love for them. Chuang Tzu would have been disappointed in me. This pain is the price that the Tai Chi person must pay for loving the world. Barbara was the cherry blossom whose beauty touched my soul and whose falling to the earth tore out my heart and shredded it with grief.

I left the class and went to the hospital. I entered the door of her room and there was Barbara lying in her bed, looking into my eyes. The moment I had dreaded ever since her phone call was here. The first thing she said to me was, 'Why this?' What could I say? I felt so helpless and my heart was being torn apart. I tried to think of some kind of rational explanation but whenever I looked into her eyes awaiting my answer, all my philosophy collapsed. Finally, my soul sank into the Wu Chi and there in that ocean of love my answer came floating out, an answer not formed in rational thought but in poetry, the language of love.

Death is a mystery and thus it cannot be grasped by the rational mind. Lao Tzu and the Taoists do not say what comes after death for they do not 'know' and cannot 'know'. Hence, there was no rational answer to give Barbara. When rationality and the mind are stopped, that leaves only poetry and the heart. Only the heart can speak of mystery. My answer to Barbara was not 'truth', for who knows what that is? Certainly, not I. What I gave was a pretty answer; an answer that flowed from the heart and tried to convey love and compassion. In the same way that what I write in this book may not be true, the idea of a loving life leading toward oneness may not be true, but it is pretty, so why not? I tell my students that they are becoming real Tai Chi people not when they do the Tai Chi movements perfectly but when even their mistakes are pretty and flowing. It is the same in life. When you make a mistake that was based in love, people will resent your mistake much less because it was 'pretty' (that is, arising from love).

Thus, I told Barbara that the Tao had looked down upon my struggles and took pity upon my loneliness. Seeing my suffering, the Mother Tao called some of her favourite stars from the heavens and sent them down to be my students. But Mother Tao missed her most beautiful star and had now called for it to come home and take its place again in the heavens so that its beauty can be shared again with all.

Hence, I learned a great lesson from Barbara. I learned that death is the poetical fulfilment of life and that, as with life, death must be met with the love and beauty of the Wu Chi nature. Thus, I bow to my teacher, Barbara Schmid.

Chapter 17

Tao Chia and Tao Chiao

The world is ruled by letting things take their course.
It cannot be ruled by interfering.

VERSE 48

The world of ego is like a malignant growth, destroying all that it touches. It is a leech that sucks the soul out of all things and leaves nothing but an empty shell. Sacredness and meaning disappear in its presence. The Oriental arts which are so filled with meaning are also being destroyed. Karate ceased being the Way of Justice and Honour when it became a competition where the students seek to win medals. Yoga ceased to be the Way of Oneness with God when people came to it to lose weight and stay youthful.

Tai Chi is also dying in the overwhelming presence of the ego world. People who have done Tai Chi for years tell me that they have never heard of the things that are written of in this book and they ask me why. And, if a person who is interested in learning Tai Chi visits several Tai Chi schools, there is very little chance that he will be told of the Wu Chi aspect and its vital importance to Tai Chi. Tai Chi is becoming a business where the students pay their money, sign a contract, learn a movement and go home having had their exercise for the week. The Tai Chi teacher is becoming merely a businessman like any other merchant. How did this happen to something so full of beauty and meaning as Tai Chi? To find the answer, we must look at the very beginning of Taoist philosophy in China.

It is the fear of death, pain and suffering that give rise to the world of ego. The world of ego must destroy all meaning since it sees death as meaningless. If it accepted meaning in anything, then perhaps it would have to accept that death also has meaning as a natural aspect of the complete life. This, in turn, would mean that death is not to be feared or fled from.

Since the rational mind can see nothing but facts, and facts in isolation have no meaning, it sees meaning in nothing. Hence, the world of ego destroys the 'sacredness' of all that it touches. This is true for Tai Chi also and is the reason for my writing this book. The world of ego began to destroy the beauty and meaning of Taoist philosophy almost as soon as that philosophy was formulated.

From 500 BC, China was torn apart in the Warring States Period. The old empire had collapsed and every petty state was struggling to see which one would be able to gain control and create its own empire. For 200 years wars raged back and forth with extreme cruelty and destruction. It was 200 years of constant death and violence. The sages began to ask 'What is the Way of Humanity', 'How can people live together in peace and harmony?' Thus began the 'Blooming of the Hundred Flowers', or the founding of the various Chinese philosophical schools.

The Legalist school insisted that the formulation of laws dealing with all aspects of life and extreme punishment for disobeying those laws would force humans to live in peace with one another. The school of the Confucianists insisted that once humans were instructed in good moral behaviour, everything would be well. Other schools arose to offer yet other various ways.

The 'Tao Chia' (School of Taoist Philosophers) said that all these ways were crazy. You cannot separate humans from Nature and from the universe around them. There is no 'Way of Humanity' but only 'the Way' and that way is the same for all things that exist, elephants, rocks, stars, trees and people. Animals, trees and stars do not have wars because they follow their nature; they do what is natural. If human beings simply follow their nature like the rest of the universe, then peace and harmony will be realized. The nature of human beings is love and compassion. Thus love and compassion is the Tao and when we follow the love and compassion which naturally flow from our inner self, harmony and tranquillity automatically follow. If we do not interfere, everything will follow its natural course and the peace of the Tao will be present.

Hence, Taoist thought and its discipline, Tai Chi, follow the doctrine of 'Wu Wei', or letting things work out their own destinies naturally. The Tai Chi person does not act upon the world but simply flows in cooperation with the unfolding of the Wu Chi's love. Lao Tzu writes,

Therefore the sage goes about doing nothing. . .
Verse 2

and,

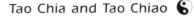

Tao abides in non-action,
Yet nothing is left undone.

Verse 37

and,

He helps the Ten Thousand Things find their
    own nature,
But refrains from action.

Verse 64

and,

Stillness and tranquillity set things in
    order in the universe.

Verse 45

In other words, to be one with the universe, you do not have to do anything. You must stop *doing* things and simply be yourself, allowing your loving Wu Chi nature to flow spontaneously. This adherence to the doctrine of Wu Wei gives the Tai Chi person a great sense of liberation as they free themselves from the petty quarrels of human society and return to the oneness of the Tao.

However, this gentle, loving, natural Way of the Tao Chia, which this book is seeking to pass on, was soon attacked by the world of ego. This attack on the meaning of Taoism and Tai Chi came in the form of the Tao Chiao (Taoist religion). The Tao Chiao arose from the innumerable hermits, alchemists and magicians seeking immortality who made their appearance at the beginning of Chinese history.

In Chinese thinking, there was no concept of the soul. Thus, for those who feared death, the natural conclusion of life, the only answer was to seek immortality in the body. Rather than seeking to cooperate with Nature in its flow, these 'adepts' or 'Feng Shih' practised 'Wu' magic, which was an effort to gain mastery over Nature by manual operations. They sought to become immortal through certain meditations, physical exercises, the taking of drugs, Yogic breathing exercises, sexual techniques and expeditions sent in search of the 'Isles of the Immortals'. They hoped that by eating certain substances or doing certain exercises their bodies would be preserved and they would thus become 'Hsien' or Immortals. They did not seek to become one with the Tao but rather to control the Tao for their own uses.

Because Taoist thinking embraces all people and does not judge or condemn, these 'adepts' flocked to Taoism and soon overwhelmed the Tao Chia thinkers by sheer numbers. The Tai Chi movements became just another tool in their desperate attempts to avoid death. Students gathered around the masters who claimed to have become immortal. The only problem was that these immortals kept dying. When this happened, the master's body was carried to some desolate spot in the middle of the night and secretly buried. The elders of the school would then announce to the other students that the master had ascended to heaven to become one of the Immortals. To confess that the master had died would admit the emptiness of the school's claim to 'knowledge'.

This problem of dying masters disappeared with the coming of

Buddhism to China. Buddhism had originally had no concept of the 'soul', but by the time it reached China, Buddhism included the soul in the teachings of certain sects. Unfortunately, the Buddhist soul disappears into Nirvana at death. There is no survival of the individual as such. Now, the Tao Chiao people were able to abandon the effort to make the body immortal. Instead, they would seek to make the soul that the Buddhists talked about immortal. Soon Tao Chiao writings appeared, such as *The Secret of the Golden Flower* which instructed the student in the methods used to build the 'immortal spirit body'. With these 'soul building' techniques, the ego could survive death.

How far away all this was from the original natural way taught by Lao Tzu. Ideas of love and compassion were lost and replaced by an isolated, egotistical search for the means of prolonging life. This invasion of Tai Chi by the world of ego destroyed all meaning, leaving only the empty shell, the Tai Chi movements. Tai Chi students travelled around China seeking fighting competitions to see who was the best fighter. Children were sent away to the mountains to spend their childhood learning from the immortal masters. Students spent years doing various breathing exercises, eating special diets, learning to knock people down with their Chi without moving, and so on.

The natural way of simply being oneself, rooted in the love of one's Wu Chi nature and flowing with the Tao, disappeared and Wu Wei was forgotten. Teachers and schools became essential in order to undergo the years of complex training required to prolong one's life.

To illustrate, a Tao Chiao story would go like this: An old master was walking along a river when he was attacked by 40 bandits. Raising his Chi energy to his fullest level, he easily defeated them all. . . or by using the fantastic leaping ability he had practised for the last 50 years, he leaped to the roof of a temple where the bandits could not reach him.

The Tao Chia version of the story would be: an old master was walking alone by a river when he was attacked by 40 bandits, but so much love and compassion shone from his being that the hard souls of the bandits were melted by his warmth and beauty and they could not bring themselves to harm him.

When Tai Chi arrived in the Western world, the idea of seeking immortality lost its power to attract people to Tai Chi. Most Westerners come from a Christian background and already believe they possess an immortal soul. If they do not believe in the Christian immortal soul, there is very little chance that they would accept a Chinese concept of building a soul.

Thus, Tai Chi changed its claims about immortality when it came to the West, and instead spoke of long life and good health. It was the Oriental world of ego meeting the Western world of ego. Tai Chi has become popular in the Western world because, like the other aspects of Western life, it has no meaning. In the world of ego, life is meaningless. The whole purpose of life is simply to avoid death for as long as possible and this is what a meaningless Tai Chi will help you do.

Lao Tzu, too, speaks of long life. He writes,

That which goes against the Tao comes to
    an early end.

                        Verse 30

And, in Verse 59, he writes of 'the Tao of long life'. But what he means by 'long life' is completely different from what the Tao Chiao people were seeking. To Lao Tzu, long life means a life that is long enough to fulfil one's destiny. His concern is that one not meet an 'early end'. Thus, a 'long' life only has meaning if the students are one with the love of their Wu Chi nature and are flowing with the Tao toward their own destiny in the Whole. The number of years that one lives has no meaning otherwise. When your destiny is fulfilled, it is time to go and it does not matter if that is in six months, 20 years or 120 years.

The vast majority of Tai Chi schools in the West (and probably in China, too) are from this Tao Chiao tradition and that is why it is very difficult to find a school that speaks of the things written in this book, and the average Tai Chi teacher has never heard of Tao Chiao or Tao Chia. That is why Tai Chi advertisements describe Tai Chi as healing gymnastics or longevity exercises.

Once, I was sitting at a table at an outdoor restaurant wearing a shirt with a Tao symbol on it. A young woman sat down at my table and told me that she had studied Tai Chi for six years and she wanted me to know that the Yin and Yang symbols on my shirt were flowing in the wrong direction. I immediately realized that she was from the Tao Chiao. What concerned her was that the emblem on my shirt was flowing the wrong way, not whether I was a warm, loving human being, or not.

Usually, I get sick with a cold or the flu once a year. People often ask me how a Tai Chi teacher can get sick. After all, Tai Chi is for health and long life. These are Tao Chiao people. They reject illness as they reject death. But nowhere in *The Tao Te Ching* does Lao Tzu reject illness. In fact, the Tai Chi person rejects nothing. Everything is the Tai Chi person's teacher, including illness. My once-a-year illness is my soul's way of making me slow down and turn inward.

When I am ill, I become very quiet and I withdraw from the outer senses. This automatically turns me inward toward an experience of the present state of my inner self. Some of my most educating spiritual insights have come during these periods of illness. I would hate to give them up. Any Tai Chi system will give you good health, but if that is all that the students are seeking, that is all that they will find and the heart of Tai Chi will be lost to them.

This invasion and domination of Tai Chi by the world of ego is the reason I have written this book and my first book, *The Tai Chi Journey*. It will be hard for the student to find a school that will teach true Tai Chi, but it does not matter. Any school will teach you movements that will help you become one with your body and preserve your health. You can be your own teacher and teach yourself the 'Way' by holding to the true meaning of Tai Chi expressed by Lao Tzu. Learn your movements and keep to the ancient Way. Live the true essence of Tai Chi and do not become misled into believing that the movements themselves are Tai Chi. Lao Tzu writes,

Therefore the truly great man dwells on what
is real and not what is on the surface,
on the fruit and not the flower.

Verse 38

283

The Yin of Tai Chi

and,

> Those that know me are few;
> Those that abuse me are honoured.
> Therefore the sage wears rough clothing and
>   holds the jewel in his heart.

Verse 70

Chapter 18

Last Words

The Yin of Tai Chi

The universe is sacred.

VERSE 29

The universe is sacred. It is a oneness created from love, consisting of love and flowing toward love. All it wants is to love you and to be with you. Every tree, every blade of grass, every rock, every animal, every person is your child who calls to your soul for nourishment. You are the Tai Chi person with an endless source of love at your centre. You are the Jian who tends to the needs of everything in your garden.

Humans have destroyed the sacred world. We have polluted the rivers, cut down the forests, dug up the mountains, killed animals for sport and severed our kinship with Nature. The Tai Chi person is the Earth Father or Earth Mother who seeks to recapture the sacredness and the awe of the ancient Mother World that blossomed forth from the Wu Chi's love. It is you, the Tai Chi person, who must make the rivers sing again, who must touch the trees with your soul so that there are once again sacred groves, who must give poetry back to human beings.

The only reason to do Tai Chi is because your loving heart is torn open by the pain, suffering and weeping of the world. When true Tai Chi people feel this overwhelming pain in their heart, they have no

The Yin of Tai Chi

choice but to hold the world close and let their Father-Mother love bring its warm, caressing healing to all things. Thus, to be a Tai Chi person is not a decision, but rather an overpowering need to let the love of your Wu Chi nature flow toward the universe.

Tai Chi is a surrender to the constant tugging at the heart made by that vast ocean of love that is the Tao washing continuously against it. Lao Tzu writes,

> Surrender yourself humbly; then you can be
> trusted to care for all things.
> Love the world as your own self; then you
> can truly care for all things.
>
> Verse 13

In your efforts to live a life of love, you will stumble and fall many times. You will be forced to look at the negative, petty aspects of yourself. This will depress you and drag you down. But, if you endure, the glory and the beauty of a life lived in a universe where everything is alive and filled with sacredness will be yours. The spirits of all things will speak to your soul, the universe will come laughing to meet you and the world will stand in awe of your beauty. As you pass, people will be comforted by your love and the 'jewel' in your heart will light your way. You will be you and there is no more beautiful thing in the universe than you.

When your destiny is fulfilled and you return to the Great Void of the Wu Chi, you will have left behind the world of the loving Mother. Humanity and Nature will once again join together in the celebration of the sacred.

So, now I am at the end of my story that Lao Tzu began over 2,000 years ago. You, the Tai Chi student, will write more chapters with your life than Lao Tzu and I ever dreamed of. If this book helps you in the dark hours of your journey to remember the beauty of who you are and the glory that awaits you, then it will have been worth the writing. The book makes no claim to truth or understanding. It does not seek to touch your mind, but rather is only a poem written from the world of Tai

Chi to your heart. If you could prove to me that everything I have written is false, I would write it anyway because it is 'pretty'. The world of ego may trample us under its feet like the falling cherry blossom, but the stars have seen our beauty and they will remember the glory that was our lives.

May the Tao always be with you.

Bibliography

Belanger, J D, *The Place Called Attar*, Countryside Publications, Withee, Wisconsin, 1990

Carr-Gomm, Philip, *The Druid Way*, (This edition currently out of print.) Element Books Limited, Shaftesbury, 1993

Feng, Gia-fu and English, Jane, *Tao Te Ching*, Vintage Books, New York, 1989

Gadon, Elinor W, *The Once and Future Goddess*, Harper and Row Publishers, New York, 1989

Needham, Joseph, *Science and Civilisation in China*, Vol. II, Cambridge University Press, 1956

Sjö, Monica and Mor, Barbara, *The Great Cosmic Mother*, HarperCollins Publishers, New York, 1987

Walker, Barbara G, *The Woman's Encyclopedia of Myths and Secrets*, HarperCollins Publishers, New York, 1983

Index